DATE DUE			

Sarmiento in the United States

Domingo Faustino Sarmiento

Sarmiento in the United States

Elda Clayton Patton

*Visiting lecturer of Spanish
The University of Evansville*

The University of Evansville Press
Evansville, Indiana

iii

982
P21s
99321
Nov, 1976

Library of Congress Catalog Card Number 76-7319
The University of Evansville Press   Evansville, Indiana 47702
©1976 by The University of Evansville
Published 1976
Printed in The United States of America

CONTENTS

On ne tue point les idées

Sarmiento

PREFACE

For several years this book has been awaiting a propitious time for publication. I had hoped to publish it simultaneously both in Argentina and in the United States, since I wrote it to promote better understanding between our countries. However, I am advised that the publication of a book about Sarmiento is not now timely in Argentina. The very clements that Sarmiento opposed are again powerful and are keeping the country in anarchy and terror. But Sarmiento's ideals are still alive and need to be implemented if Argentina is to achieve the greatness that he foresaw.

We are very myopic concerning our Latin American neighbors. While we have our sights focused far away on the East and the West, we are oblivious to the politics to the south of us. At best, we are indifferent, believing that the other Americans are in another orbit and not worthy even of adequate news coverage. So we are unable to grasp the true significance of the political events in Latin America. The major news events are the sensational, and they are presented in ways that cause the reader to lose any interest he might have to learn more about the problems confronting those countries.

My learning Spanish opened a new world for me. I was able to read other newspapers and books and to know the problems of other young nations. Thus I became interested in Sarmiento, since he was often quoted in the leading newspapers of Buenos Aires. However, even his name activated the forces of censorship. A lecture I was invited to give about him had to be submitted in advance, and when I gave it, a policeman was present.

Many learned men of Argentina encouraged me to write of the influence that the United States had upon Sarmiento. A visit to the United States by a modern educator, Alfredo Ghioldi, had inspired him also, and it was at a lecture that he gave of his impressions that our friendship began. He spoke so kindly of my country that I was moved to tears. He became my mentor and source of much of the material in this book. I am pleased to be able to publish this book while he is living and embued with his indomitable belief that Argentina will eventually become what Sarmiento so clearly saw more than one hundred years ago. Other great men, similarly embued with Sarmiento's ideals, are no longer with us, but they are remembered among my many dear friends who commended me for my interest in Sarmiento and urged me to help Argentina by writing about him. Among them are the late Vincente Barbieri, poet; Ricardo Rojas, the dean of Argentina's writers, who said that I had a Latin soul and who was the first to bring the Nobel Prize to Argentina; Dr. B. A. Houssay; and Juan Ramón Jiménez, the Spanish poet, also a Nobel Laureate.

Many years ago Argentina was a leading agricultural producer of the world. It exported meat and grain to its Latin American neighbors, to England and to other European countries. The great land owners became wealthy, lived abroad and gave little thought to their home country and its problems in a world with rapidly increasing industrial needs. Industrialization by the State at the expense of agriculture led to the country's loss of the food markets and the loss of capital, which the absentee owner had taken to Europe, and it led also to the current inflation and meat shortages in the country, which earlier had the highest meat consumption in the world, a daily average of one kilogram per person.

The lack of leadership during the recent decades, the economic ruin and 200 percent inflation, the anarchy, terror, kidnapping and murder have created the present dismal situation in the country of which Sarmiento was president from 1868 to 1872. However, Argentina is still one blessed by rich natural resources, great expanse of land with deep top soil, a favorable location with a climate largely temperate, extending from the tropics to the Antarctic, and a literate people. How can Argentina ever become a stable democratic nation? Surely there must arise leadership to raise Argentina to her rightful place in the world, as Sarmiento hoped.

** ** ** ** ** ** ** ** **

I wish to express my gratitude to many friends who have encouraged me and helped me prepare the manuscript for publication. The untimely death of Dr. Vera Beck, who had assisted me in proofing and rewriting, has been a grievous loss to me. Others who have encouraged me are my colleagues, Drs. Edward Blumenkranz, Richard Frenkel and Roy Hart. Harrison E. Salisbury, Pulitizer Prize winning author, world authority in foreign affairs and an editor emeritus of the New York Times, has honored me by reading the manuscript and writing the introduction. Finally I wish to thank Dr. Ralph Olmsted, who has helped me in many ways.

Elda Clayton Patton, M.D.

New York January 1, 1976

INTRODUCTION

The name of Domingo Faustino Sarmiento is a banner of democracy and a rallying-point for anti-fascism in Latin America and particularly in his native Argentine. Would that it were so well known in the United States, which he saw as the model for the emerging nations of South America.

The time seems particularly appropriate for the study of Sarmiento. He liked to think of himself as the Abraham Lincoln of the Argentine, and in selecting the martyred North American president as his ideal, he told much of himself and of his philosophy of government.

Sarmiento was born deep in the back country of the Argentine on February 14, 1811. All of his life was a struggle, but never more so than in his early years as he fought to get an education, sought to evolve a view of himself and of the isolated world which surrounded him, and gradually began to develop those principles of education and democracy which were to dominate his life and to which he would devote his life.

The Argentine — indeed all of Latin America — in the days of his youth was a backwater world, far removed from the swift currents of evolutionary and revolutionary thought which had swirled up from the American and French revolutions, but not so far removed that the movement for liberating the South American continent from Spanish rule did not sweep like wildfire from one part of the vast area to another.

But what was to follow? It was easier to overthrow the weakened Spanish power than it was to evolve a new Latin state. And this was where Sarmiento's genius came into play. From the earliest moments he was convinced that education must be the foundation stone of free government and a free citizenry. He was a brilliant writer and he put his pen at the service of his ideas. For years his pen and his political ideas caused him to be exiled from the Argentine, then, as so many times in the future, in the hands of a military dictatorship.

It was in political exile in Chile in the early 1840's that Sarmiento wrote his classic *Facundo, civilización y barbarie*, a study of Facundo Quiroga, a semi-barbaric military *caudillo* of San Juan. It was the first (and long the only) socio-political study of the phenomenon of the military dictatorship in the Argentine. It was also the first Argentine book to win world renown — being translated into English, German, French and Italian.

Sarmiento travelled widely in Europe and in the United States, seeking new ideas in the broader world which could be applied to his native land. It was in the United States that he found what he felt was the Rosetta Stone of contemporary government: Popular Education. He fell under the sway of the teachings of Horace Mann, met Horace Mann and his wife in Boston, spent much time studying Mann's ideas and developing them for use in Latin America. It is from this that grew his slogan "to govern is to educate," and it was this characteristic which, in time, led him upon being elected to the highest office in Argentina to being called "the schoolmaster President".

Sarmiento was in the United States when he was elected and did not know he had been chosen until his boat put in on the way back to Buenos Aires at Rio de Janiero. The year was 1868, and he had spent the previous three years in the United States ostensibly as his country's ambassador, actually as a student of American customs, morals and achievements, travelling to almost every part of the country and investigating almost every kind of life.

He was no blind admirer of the United States. He saw its faults as clearly as anyone, particularly those stemming from excessive preoccupation with material rewards. The United States was, he understood, a land of moral contradictions. The whole country was engaged in a struggle to accumulate capital to establish itself and enter upon new enterprises. In the struggle people did not always remember moral principles. He was deeply disturbed by lynch law, widespread both in the slave states of pre-Civil War and in the Wild West. But he found other qualities which overbalanced these defects — the constant movement of younger people to the frontier, the expansion of the land in which virtually all distinctions of rank or position disappeared and the strength of religious feeling.

But most compelling of all, in Sarmiento's view, was the influence of New England, of the Puritan descendants, their tradition of hard manual labor — the Puritan work ethic. He reckoned that there were more than a million families in the United States descended from what he called "that noble stock", and it was this group which, in his opinion, provided the incentive for popular education, popular elections as well as great schemes of colonization, the building of railroads, the establishment of banks and social institutions.

In his enthusiasm Sarmiento hoped to transplant the best of America's inventions onto Latin soil in the Argentine. The widow of Horace Mann, excited by his enthusiasm, exclaimed: "You are not a man but a nation!"

Mrs. Mann's exclamation was not far from the truth. When in time Sarmiento returned to the Argentine as President he laid the foundation for a popular public education system, for the immigration and settlement of new lands, for commerce, agriculture, transport and communications. He served as president for six years — 1868-1874 — and lived on another 14 years, advising and supporting those forces which sought to elevate the plane of Argentine public life.

It seems no accident that a man with the enthusiasms, the ideals and the aspirations of Sarmiento would be controversial to this day. Sarmiento stood for morality and goodness in public life. He believed that if the people were educated they would choose worthy leaders and support sound public policy. He saw Argentina as a great nation of the world and a leader in the Latin continent. He was not merely interested in the Argentine: his interests ranged over neighboring countries, and in his long exile in Chile he took a direct hand in the politics of that state.

Sarmiento's ideas are not likely to be popular with those who seek to rule by appeals to emotion and personal greed; by those who rule by force or threat; by inciters to violence and angry rhetoric. The atmosphere of Latin politics today would hardly be congenial to Sarmiento. There were those in his time who criticized him for his lavish acceptance of the U.S. model. There would be more critics were he alive to advocate that policy today. Yet, if one goes back to the days of the 1840's and 1850's and 1860's, one can see that policies which are taken for granted today were bold and innovative in the America of that time.

Today in the Argentine Sarmiento is not published. He is not cited by the dictatorial rulers. His name is under a ban. And for good reason. It stands for decency, honesty and an optimistic view of the world. This hardly seems radical today. Nor did it in his own day — except among those who stand at the opposite poles. The hatred of Sarmiento in Latin American circles is a measure of the distance which must be travelled to get back to first principles. And Sarmiento's name and principles could well be studied in the land where he found his ideals. We too could take a lesson from Sarmiento's early ideals and enthusiasms.

Harrison E. Salisbury

PART ONE
Chapter I
PLAN AND SOURCES

During my assignment in the United States Embassy in Buenos Aires, Argentina from 1945 to 1947, I became so interested in Sarmiento due to the countless references to him in the brilliant editorials of *La Prensa* and *La Nación* that I decided to ask for a leave of absence in order to study this great leader of the past century. The dramatic political experiment that Argentina is now (1950) experiencing finds Sarmiento as the chief issue — those who shout, "Death to Sarmiento" only prove that Sarmiento and his ideas live.

My story is to tell of the influence the United States had upon Sarmiento during his two visits here. No visitor has honored the United States more than he, for while there are many who have admired the United States, it is safe to say that few have returned to their countries imbued with such enthusiasm to put into practice the ideas which characterize the United States, as did Sarmiento.

The plan of my book is first to describe the Argentina which was Sarmiento's, with the *pampa*, the *gaucho*, Buenos Aires and the historical background of the time. For this I have used as sources, *Facundo*, the most powerful of all of Sarmiento's works; *Far Away and Long Ago*, by William Henry Hudson; *A History of the Argentine Republic* by F. A. Kirkpatrick; *A History of Argentina* by Ricardo Levene; *Argentina, Brazil and Chile Since Independence* by J. F. Rippy; *History of the Latin-American Nations* by W. S. Robertson; *Buenos Aires and the Provinces of the River Plate*; by Sir Woodbine Parish; *Martín Fierro* by José Hernández; *Amalia* by José Mármol; *Una excursión a los indios ranqueles* by Lucio V. Mansilla.

For the brief summary of the life and works of Sarmiento, I have found my material mostly in *Mi defensa, Recuerdos de*

provincia and *Dominguito* from the *Obras* of Sarmiento. I have
also used *El profeta de la pampa* and *El pensamiento vivo de
Sarmiento* by Ricardo Rojas. Professor Rojas was also very helpful
to me during my stay in Argentina. *Sarmiento, la vida, la obra, las
ideas, el genio* and *The Pan American Ideals of Sarmiento* by
Alberto Palcos have also been used. I also had the opportunity to
know Professor Palcos, who was also very helpful to me while in
Buenos Aires.

For the last chapter of the first part, "Travels Through Europe
and Africa Enroute to the United State," I have used as the most
important source Sarmiento's *Viajes* which comprise *Volume* V of
the *Obras* of Sarmiento. In addition I have used *Páginas confidenciales de Domingo F. Sarmiento* by Alberto Palcos. In my
opinion it is necessary to trace the long itinerary and the impressions which his travels had upon him before reaching the
United States in order to show the great variety of experiences
which resulted from Sarmiento's visit to United States and the
mental outlook which Sarmiento had from his travels in the Old
World as contrasted with what he found in the United States. Here
was the turning point in his thinking. Before seeing the United
States in 1847, Sarmiento had focused his attention upon France
and the ideas of the French Revolution, but after the visit to
Europe and to the United States, Sarmiento looked to the United
States.

For the first chapter of the second part, First Visit to the
United States, I have again used as the chief source, *Viajes*. Here
Sarmiento has given his impressions in a lengthy letter to his
friend, Don Valentín Alsina, found in *Viajes* pp. 344 - 440 and
Incidentes de viaje pp. 440 - 514. The work is especially important
since it is the first one published by an Argentine about the United
States, and even though more than a hundred years have passed
since, this important work still maintains its interest and freshness
in describing the United States of 1847.

In succeeding chapters I have again used *Viajes* in giving the
impressions which Sarmiento had of his visit in the United States
and the influence the visit had upon him.

For the "Second Visit to the United States," I have used
several volumes of the *Obras*, especially XXIX, XXXIV, XXXV,
XXXVIII, XXXIX, IL along with Rojas', *El profeta de la pampa,
Sarmiento — Mitre Correspondencia, Epistolario entre Sarmiento y
Posse, Boletín de la Academia Argentina de Letras*, for the letters

of Sarmiento to Mrs. Horace Mann, the originals of which I was also permitted to see in the National Library in Buenos Aires. Thanks to the kind assistance of Mr. Lysando Galtier, I was permitted to work in the archives of the Ministry of Foreign Affairs, where I worked upon the original reports that Sarmiento sent while in the United States as Minister. I was also given help in the General Archives of the Nation, the Archives of the Mitre Museum. I should like to mention the assistance which Dr. Allison William Bunkley generously gave me during his last visit to Argentina before his untimely death.

For the chapters treating Sarmiento's "Impressions of the Second Visit," I have again used chiefly the *Obras*, XXIX, *Boletín de la Academia Argentina de Letras*, for Sarmiento's letters to Mary Mann, and *Páginas confidenciales de Domingo F. Sarmiento* by Alberto Palcos.

For the chapter concerning the "Influence of the Second Visit," I have used the *Obras*, IL, XXI, XXXV, XXXVIII, and XXXIX. The Conclusion is based upon sources already mentioned, especially Rojas, *El profeta de la pampa*, and a letter of the head of the Mitre Museum, Mr. Narciso Margues.

Chapter II
SARMIENTO'S ARGENTINA

1. The Pampa

The territory which comprises Argentina extends from the lush, verdant, tropical zone to the barren, bleak, frigid zone but the part which provides the sustenance of the national life is the *pampa*. This typical Argentina, for it is the region which has become most popularized in the thought concerning Argentina, is characterized by the vast plain of the pampa, stoneless and tree-less, level to the eye but sloping up imperceptibly from the Atlantic ocean to the Andes mountains.

> So vast is the extent of the pampas that, in the north, they are bounded by palm groves and, in the south, by the eternal snows.[1]

The *pampa* was beautiful. It was covered with the tall, coarse pampa grass, high enough to hide the wild deer and quail that roamed the open country. In spring the thistle flowered and in midsummer it turned to seed that fed the herds of cattle and sheep or the wild birds of the marshes. Where there were houses men planted trees for shade and fruit: willows and poplars, acacias, pears, nectarines, apricots and peaches. Such groves stood out prominently on the flat, monotonous *pampa* and marked the lonely ranch house of the dweller. Best of all was the *ombú*. The *ombú* is part of the legend that is Argentina and when the criollo built his hut on the plain, it was beside a friendly *ombú*. Rarely does one see a nest in the *ombú* for its leaves are said to be noxious at night. And that is why it would never occur to a *gaucho* to sleep beneath it.

The *estancia* of William Henry Hudson, who, though writing in

English, was yet one of the most authentic of all the Argentine novelists, was called *Los Veinticinco Ombúes* — The Twenty-Five Ombúes. Hudson has described the Argentina as he remembered it in his youth:

> The undulating country had been left behind; before us and on both sides the land, far as one could see, was absolutely flat, everywhere green with the winter grass, but flowerless at that season, and with the gleam of water over the whole expanse. It had been a season of great rains, and much of the flat country had been turned into shallow lakes. That was all there was to see, except the herds of cattle and horses and an occasional horseman galloping over the plain, and the sight at long distances of a grove or small plantation of trees, marking the site of an estancia or sheep and cattle farm, these groves appearing like islands on the sealike flat country.[2]

Sarmiento who wrote without having seen the *pampa* until years later, gives us a vivid description of this vast expanse of territory and the life of the *gaucho* there:

> The immense expanse of land, which at its extremes is entirely unpopulated, possesses navigable rivers that the fragile little boat has not yet plowed through. The ailment that afflicts the Argentine Republic is spaciousness; the desert surrounds it everywhere, as is insinuated in its innermost recesses; solitude, depopulated without a single human dwelling, are in general the unquestionable boundaries between some provinces and others. Out there, immensity everywhere; the plain immense, the forests immense, the rivers immense, the horizon always uncertain, ever becoming jumbled with the earth amid varicolored clouds and delicate vapors which in the distant view do not mark the point where the world ends and the sky begins. (VII, 19)[3]

It was a land rich in potentialities when Sarmiento wrote these lines from his exile in Chile. But none realized more than he how poor was the present. There was not a single highway, not a single railroad in a million square miles. The country was watered by navigable rivers; there was not a single boat, not a single bridge. From Salta in the north to Buenos Aires in the south goods and

men came by oxcart, taking three months for the trip. The soil
was as rich as it is now, with three to eleven feet of alluvial top
soil, and fertilizers were unknown to the Argentines. Yet the
owners of the *estancias* (ranches) imported flour from the United
States and men whose cattle numbered thousands had neither milk
nor butter to eat.

It was a land of sudden death. A man might die from crossing
the southern frontier into the Indian country. He might die in a
drunken fight with knives in a country tavern. He might die in civil
war. Every province had its *gaucho* army and some had two. Life
was not sacred, nor was it comfortable. In Buenos Aires, the
dictator Juan Manuel de Rosas set the style for *caudillos*, and one
might be stabbed in the street or in his own house, or shot by a
firing squad. The great men of Argentina, the men who believed in
democracy, as Sarmiento and Alberdi did, or who believed in the
nation's greatness, as San Martin did, or who just did not like the
cruel Juan Manuel de Rosas, and there were many in this category,
were in exile in Chile, in Uruguay and in France.

2. The Gaucho

The *gaucho* is not the original inhabitant of the *pampa* but
rather the result of the meeting of the Spanish conqueror with the
native Indian. In the 16th century, the *gaucho* was then an Indian
or warrior who fought all forms of civilization. The later *mestizo
or criollo* adopted the name of this Indian warrior, his manners
and customs, even his native habitat, and became equally a warrior
who fought all forms of civilization. He had to fight in order to
live; he had to fight the elements of nature, the roving bands of
animals, the Indian raids, the prairie fire and eventually, all the
forces of civilization.

Nature all about him was severe, violent and impulsive and he,
in turn, developed these qualities in order to survive. The sudden
tempestuous storms of the *pampas*, the drouths and the thunder
and lightning required hardness in the individual who dominated
them. The Indian raids were cruel and the *gaucho* became
accustomed to death and destruction. He became hardened to the
shedding of blood in his frequent butchering of the animals of his
herd, whether of necessity to satisfy his hunger or need for a new
pair of boots or simply as a target for his skill with the *boleadora
or facón*.

To Sarmiento the *gaucho* represented all that was the worst, all that was the most savage, in the Argentine character, and he called his remarkable study of the *gaucho* mentality *Facundo*; or *Civilización y barbarie*. *Facundo* was the first Argentine book to achieve fame in world letters; it was translated into French, Italian, German and English and through *Facundo*, the *pampa*, the *gaucho*, and Quiroga and Rosas acquired world fame.

The authentic *gaucho* of Sarmiento's time must have looked much like the desert nomad of the Sahara, for when Sarmiento saw the Arabs in Africa, he was amazed at how much they resembled his countrymen, both in costume and physiognomy. The rein, the whip, and the bit showed their Moorish-Andalusian descent.

It is not beyond our purpose to recall here the notable similarities that the Argentines bear to the Arabs. In Algiers, in Oran, in Nascara and in the settlements of the desert, I always saw the Arabs gathered in cafes, because it was strictly forbidden to them to use liquors, crowded around the singer, usually two of them, who accompany themselves as a duet with guitars, reciting national songs as plaintive as ours are sad. The Arab's bridle rein is woven of leather and with a whip like ours; the bit which we use is the Arab bit and many of our customs reveal the contact our forefathers had with the Moors of Andalusia. Let us not speak of faces: some Arabs I have met, I could swear I had seen in my country. (*Nota de la edición de 1850.* VII, 48)

This nomad horseman was a cross between Spanish father and Indian mother, and he had the Spaniard's dignity and the Indian's savage skills. He owned what he could wear or ride — his horses, his weapons and his clothes. Nor was Sarmiento mistaken in noting the similarity of the *gaucho* and the Arab, for the *gaucho's* clothes were burnooselike in their looseness. He wore a shirt and long white cotton drawers with a fringe at the bottom; and over his drawers went a kind of a long diaper, the *chiripá*, girdled at the waist with a sash or a leather and silver belt. This strange garment gave way to the baggy cossack trousers called *bombachas*, which were the adaptation of European exporters to the Argentine.

Besides the *gaucho* wore a short bolero jacket and, thrown over his shoulders, his *poncho* of sheep or vicuña wool. His hat was a felt *chambergo*, a strange kind of a hat with a high crown and a narrow brim; and under his hat he usually tied his long hair in a colored handkerchief. The general effect of these haphazard garments was that of trailing and ill-fitting apparel. But as a matter of fact, they were quite comfortable and useful since the *poncho* served as a raincoat or overcoat during the day and a blanket at night.

The strangest article of all was his horsehide boot made from the hide of a colt's hind leg. The skin was cut in the middle of the thigh, and again about nine inches above the fetlock, and was stripped off. The upper part formed the boot's leg, the hock fitted over the heel, and the rest covered the foot, leaving the big toe showing. This boot was fitted to the man's leg while it was still moist and it took the form of the foot when dry. The big toe remained free so that the horseman could grasp the stirrup, which might be the usual kind or a bone dangling on a leather thong.

The *gaucho* lived in the saddle. Layer upon layer of blankets and sheepskins, topped by two hard leather cylinders that lie on either side provided a very bulky saddle and forced the rider to bend his knees almost as if he were in a chair. Coiled across the saddle was the lasso, an important article for the *gaucho*, along with his *facón* and *bolas*. The *facón* served as the knife to strip the hide from the cows, to cut the choice bits out for roasting and also for fighting. After a few drinks at the country tavern, he was ready to challenge anyone to a duel. The *bolas* were two or three leather-covered stones which are tied together by thongs and whirled rapidly over the head and shot at the feet of an animal, to throw it, or at the head to kill it. This instrument, an invention of the Indians, was also used in the civil wars. The *boleada* was an animal or ostrich hunt by a group of riders who formed a circle and closed in, killing those trapped. In theory this sport was limited to game but often in the excitement of the chase, cattle and horses belonging to others were included in the slaughter. At night the hunters gathered around a campfire to drink *mate* and play the guitar and sing. *Mate*, the green tea from Paraguay, which is drunk from a gourd through a silver tube provided the only variant to the strict beef diet.

The *gaucho* mentality was as primitive as the environment that formed it. Life in the open developed physical qualities without any corresponding intellectual ones. The habit of surmounting obstacles and of constantly defying and conquering nature developed the *gaucho's* feeling of individual superiority and self-importance. He was strong, proud, and energetic. Uneducated, but without the need for an education, lacking both a livelihood and necessities, he was happy in his poverty, which he did not consider as such, never having known any other mode of life. His hatred for the educated man is implacable and his disgust for his clothes, habits, and manners insurmountable. Sarmiento has described this hatred of the *gaucho* for the city man perfectly:

> . . . it is necessary to see these faces covered with beards, the grave, serious expressions like those of the Asiatic Arabs, to judge the compassionate disdain the sight of the sedentary man from the cities inspires in them, a man who may have read many books but does not know how to terrify an untamed bull and kill him, who probably does not know how to provide himself with a horse in open country, on foot and with nobody's help, who has never stopped a tiger, faced his attack with his dagger in one hand and his poncho wrapped in the other while he pierces its heart and leaves it lying at his feet. (VII, 33)

The *gaucho* had much of the child in him. Sarmiento tells one of the popular anecdotes about Facundo Quiroga and a soldier thief. A piece of property was missing and every effort to discover the guilty one had been fruitless. Facundo called his soldiers up to him and after asking the culprit to surrender, and getting no reply, he cut identical wands and gave one to each man. "Now," he said sternly, "tomorrow, I shall know who is the thief, because his wand will grow longer tonight." The following morning, he lined up his *gauchos* again, and found his man. The poor culprit, in guilty fear, had whittled off his stick during the night. This is a curious tale and shows the primitive mentality of the age, and how well Facundo and the other *caudillos* understood it. The *caudillos* inspired both devotion and fear.

As in all primitive peoples, there was a thin border line between fact and fancy, between actual reality and the dim world of spirits. Lucio V. Mansilla, who has left a remarkable record of an expedition against the Indians, tells of a soldier who was subject to hallucinations. He had once murdered the woman with whom he was living, because one night he dreamed that another man made love to her, and he became so desperate that one night he stabbed her as she lay beside him.[4]

It is not surprising that such men had to be ruled by force. Customs of this sort require vigorous methods of suppression. All that the *gaucho* had of the democratic spirit was a sense of personal liberty that was anarchy. The border line between the *gaucho* and the bad *gaucho* was doubtful. Both had probably done their share of violent killing; but one, from bad luck perhaps, had gone beyond the pale of the law. "Law" was at best a relative term. Each *caudillo* was his own law, with as much order as he could enforce. With distances so great, communication poor and the population scattered out, real organization was impossible.

The *caudillos* of the civil wars — Rosas in Buenos Aires, Facundo in La Rioja, López in Santa Fe, and all the others — were men who appealed to the superstition of the *gauchos* and to their admiration of physical skill and bravery. Sarmiento says of the *caudillo* of his country:

> The Argentine chief is a Mohammed, who at his whim could change the dominant religion and forge a new one. He has all powers; his injustice is a misfortune for his victim but is not an abuse on his part, because he can be unjust; moreover, he must necessarily be unjust, always having been so. (VII, 54)

Thus we see the heritage that was Argentina's. None more than Sarmiento realized the two rival and incompatible societies existing in Argentina. And we shall see the triumph of the *caudillos* over the cities in the personification of Rosas, who stuck the *gaucho's* knife into cultivated Buenos Aires and destroyed the work of centuries — devastating civilization, laws, and liberty.

3. The City — Buenos Aires

In the early years of the nineteenth century, Buenos Aires had little of the regal in her appearance, even though she was called the Queen of the Plata. It was a dull, flat-roofed colorless little town along the muddy banks of a muddy river. It had not even a port to receive the ships that brought it the European woolens and silks, the cutlery and ironware, the cheese, olive oil and wine. The boats anchored at high tide and as the water receded, the passengers and merchandise were unloaded in the huge wheeled oxcarts. The town, like all Spanish colonial towns, was cut into square blocks, with streets crossing each other, as prescribed by the Laws of the Indies, at every one hundred sixty yards. The buildings were one story high, of whitewashed brick or adobe, and faced each other across streets — again as set out by the Laws of the Indies — that were just ten yards wide.

Some streets were paved, but well into the middle of the century those who ventured too close to the outskirts of the city saw their animals mire down in the mud. Public hygiene was unknown. There were neither sewers nor waterworks. The better families drained water from their roofs into cisterns in the patio but the poor families had to buy water from the water carts that were pulled by oxen from door to door. Milk was peddled on horseback from large cans that hung from the sides of the saddle. It is not surprising that typhoid fever was prevalent and that there were terrible outbreaks of yellow fever even as late as the 1870's. Food, except for meat, was costly; and out of season it was scarce.

However, the population presented a colorful panorama with men in bright *ponchos*, merchants, soldiers and friars. There were all races: Indians and *mestizos*, negroes and mulattos, and pure whites. Ladies of society dressed quietly in black silk with black or white lace mantillas for mass but they carried brilliant rugs over their arms to kneel on and over their shoulders, they usually wore a colored shawl.

In spite of its quaint charm, this was the most important city of South America, and it was the economic heart of the Argentine provinces. Buenos Aires lived from its hides and salted beef. In return for the hides and tallow, the capital imported all that it used from Europe. It was a provider of raw materials and a consumer of manufactured goods. Why should the *porteño* buy his *ponchos* in Santiago del Estero when he could buy an English one for less? Or why should he buy wines made in San Juan and Mendoza when he could buy French wines for less? Why should he buy sugar and rice in Tucuman when they could be brought more quickly from Brazil? That was the problem. This was the issue that made the Revolution and the civil war between the capital city and the starving provinces. The secret of this curious situation — that the interests of Buenos Aires were directly opposed to the interests of the provinces — was transportation. Buenos Aires had access to the sea and to Europe whereas it was isolated from the interior by the vast stretches of land. So it was that Buenos Aires turned her back on the provinces and faced London and Paris. She had the finest of woolens from the English, her poetry and litera-ture from the French. And thus was born the *porteño* mentality that can be summed up as the conviction that Argentina exists for Buenos Aires and that all outside the limits of Buenos Aires is outside the limits of civilization.

To Sarmiento the city life meant civilization as contrasted with that of the *gaucho*. The Revolution succeeded in the city because there were books and ideas, a municipal spirit, courts, laws, education, and all the points of contact which we share with the European. There was a basis of organization — incomplete and backward — but precisely because it was incomplete and had not yet reached the level already known to be attainable, the revolution was enthusiastically adopted. But in the country regions, the revolution was a problem. To withdraw from the authority of the king was agreeable only insofar as it meant complete withdrawal from all authority. But the revolution was useful in the sense that it provided an outlet for the surplus energy which the *gaucho* possessed. Sarmiento is aware of the problem when he says:

The city man wears European clothing, lives the civilized life as we know it everywhere; there laws exist, ideas of progress, means of instruction, some municipal organization, the regular government, etc. Leaving the confines of the city, everything changes aspect: the country man wears other clothing, which I shall call American because it is common to all peoples; his life habits are different, his needs peculiar and limited; they appear to be two different societies, two peoples strange to each other. There is even more: the country man, far from aspiring to be like the city man, disdainfully rejects his luxuries and courteous manners; and the costume of the city man, the formal dress coat, the cape, the saddle, no European sign can present itself with impunity in the countryside. Everything civilized that exists in the city is blockaded out there, exiled to the country; and whoever should dare to appear in frock coat, for example, riding on an English saddle, would attract upon himself the mockery and brutish aggressions of the country people. (VII, 28)

4. Historical Background

Argentina looks toward Europe perhaps because unlike the other eastern countries of the Americas, she was colonized paradoxically enough from the west. Early colonization efforts by men from the Old World had failed but the Spanish settlers of Peru pushed eastward across the Andes and formed several settlements between 1551 and 1573. Mendoza, Tucumán, and Santiago del Estero were all established before Juan de Garay laid out the settlement which today forms a part of Buenos Aires, the real heart of the nation, in 1580.

These early colonists found the *pampas* well stocked with wild horses and cattle, descendants of the animals brought over by still earlier failures in colonizing Argentina. The first immigration was strengthened by more Spaniards drifting down from the northwest, and only the most daring or exceptionally strong could survive. There were always hostile Indians to fight and a discouraging trade system which offset the material advantages of the amazingly fertile soil.

The new colony was forbidden to trade directly across the Atlantic under Spain's navigation laws of that time. So it was that for 200 years the hides, tallow, and other pastoral products legally had to go by muleback through Peru, up the Pacific coast to the Isthmus of Panama, across that strip of land by muleback again and finally by ship to the mother country. Merchandise imported had to be brought back the same difficult route. This system encouraged illicit trade in wild cattle and hides which became the livelihood for the *gauchos*.

The Viceroyalty of Río de la Plata was created in 1776. Besides the present Republic of Argentina, this vast territory of nearly 2,000,000 square miles included the present republics of Paraguay, Uruguay and a part of Bolivia.

As an independent nation, Argentina dates from 1810, when a group of Argentine leaders and intellectuals, stimulated into action by the successful North American and French Revolutions, and galvanized by the repulsing of two British invasions by the Argentine militia, met in Buenos Aires on the 25th of May 1810 and proclaimed the declaration of independence. Sarmiento boasted that he was conceived during the jubilant celebrations of the Revolution of the 25th of May. This date marks the beginning of the period of emancipation and includes the movement for independence and the process of national organization.

The separatist movement of the provinces, the United Provinces of La Plata, extended from 1810 to July 9, 1816, the date upon which the Congress of Tucumán confirmed the work of the May Revolution. The revolution, which in 1816 extended throughout the former viceroyalty of the Río de la Plata, in 1817 became an American Revolution carried by General San Martín triumphantly into the neighboring countries of Chile, Peru and Ecuador. Thus it was that General José de San Martín won independence not only for Argentina, but for Chile and Peru as well. His greatest military exploit was the organizing and training, at Mendoza, of the famous Army of the Andes which he led across that range, in a march more difficult than Napoleon's crossing of the Alps, into Chile and later into Peru. It was in this army that Sarmiento's father had participated in the battle of Chacabuco and Sarmiento was proud of his father's part in the Independence.

The period of emancipation for the destinies of Spanish America closed in 1824 with the battle of Ayacucho, which marked the close of hostilities fought by the patriots against the Spanish armies on the American continent. The Argentine Revolution is a milestone in the history of free peoples. Like the Revolution in North America and the French Revolution, it was a revolution of principles; it overthrew one regime to supplant it by another, which proved to be liberal in its laws and guarantees.

The independence of the country once secured, there was then to be solved the difficult problem of national organization. After 1810, questions of government had caused various conflicts among the patriots. There was almost as much fighting among them as against the Spaniards. Since the first patriot government was the outcome of the revolution, the logical result was that the patriots were concerned as to what type of government should be adopted by the new nation. Therefore, after 1810 we see develop two lines of thought referring to the organization of the government: one represents the external action of the revolution and has as its object independence; the other represents internal action and has as its object national organization.

While the winning of independence is determined on the battlefield, the problem of political organization is of a different nature and requires the calm and mature judgment of politicians and statesmen rather than the heroism of the nameless soldiers who have made the supreme sacrifice in the name of independence. In order to form a stable political organization, it is necessary to take into consideration many factors. It is not sufficient to adopt a constitution based upon ideals but rather one that takes into account the particular country, its history and social life, the economic conditions of its peoples and their capacity for government and along with all of this, the political ideals as indicative of the course of progress.

Almost a half a century was necessary to solve the problems and complications of the political organization of Argentina. Her independence had become complete with the founding of the United Provinces of La Plata by the Congress of Tucumán in 1816. The new republic was then launched in a series of political adventures in which juntas, triumvirates, directorates, presidents, several well-defined periods of anarchy, and the 23-year dictatorship of Juan Manuel de Rosas followed each other in rapid succession. It was not until 1853 that the Argentine nation began to inaugurate constitutional presidents. During this long period, each effort to constitute or to organize the country was followed by civil wars and strife among the sister provinces. The general constituent assembly of 1815 framed several partial organic laws and formed a commission to formulate a constitutional project yet it did not promulgate a constitution. When the Congress of Tucumán in 1816 considered the political organization of the country, the majority of its members were so unstable as to favor a monarchical form of government. However this congress did not adopt a constitution until 1819 when it formed one of the unitarian or centralistic type that the people and the political leaders disobeyed. The constituent congress of 1824 also formed a centralistic constitution in 1826, which was also resisted. In 1853, the constituent congress of Santa Fe approved the federal constitution but it was not to be put into effect throughout Argentina until after the battle of Pavón in 1861, when Buenos Aires entered the confederation.

The history of the national organization might be divided into five distinct periods: that one extending from 1810 until 1820; the one from 1820 until 1829; the one from 1829 until 1852; another from 1852 until 1800 and the last one from 1880 until the present time.

The first period begins with the successive, violent crises of the patriot governments that with the exception of that of Pueyrredón, did not last for the time set by the constitution or a specific law. Thus the junta of patriotic government established on May 25, 1810 was replaced by the great junta because of the differences between President Saavedra and Secretary Moreno. The revolution of the 5th and 6th of April, 1811, drove out the followers of Moreno and formed the first triumvirate. This new body disrupted the junta of observation, a legislative group composed of the deputies who belonged to the great junta. The first triumvirate was overthrown on the 8th of October, 1812 by a revolution which installed a second triumvirate. This new body was dissolved in 1814 and the directory was organized, which represented unipersonal executive power. The first director was Gervasio Posadas, but he had to give up his office before completing his one-year term. His successor, Alvear, was overthrown in 1815 and for the first time the national government was interrupted in a transitory fashion. The Congress of Tucumán designated as supreme director, Juan Martín de Pueyrredón, who ruled for three years and restrained the outbreak of anarchy with an iron hand. After the Constitution of 1819 was promulgated, Pueyrredón resigned and anarchy broke out.

The period of 1820 to 1829 includes a study of political anarchy and of political leadership or *caudillismo*. Except for a short period during the presidency of Rivadavia, the national government was suspended and the provinces were in the hands of their respective *caudillos*.

The third period of from 1829 to 1852 comprises the twenty years of the rule of Rosas. This era represents an important stage in Argentine political and social evolution, because the political parties with principles, the federalists and centralists, caused a crisis owing to the peculiarities of social psychology and public spirit, and the international problems that arose. It was during this period that Sarmiento was forced into exile and carried on his attacks from the press in Chile against the barbaric practices of Rosas.

The fourth period of 1852 to 1880 includes the downfall of Rosas at Caseros and the conflict that began between the Province of Buenos Aires and the Argentine Confederation, represented respectively by Mitre and Urquiza, which for almost ten years kept the nation's organizations in suspense. In 1853 the Congress of Santa Fe promulgated the Argentine Constitution and constitutional presidencies were begun but without the Province of Buenos Aires, which entered the Confederation after the battle of Pavón in 1861. After the revolts of 1874 and 1880 were suppressed, national organization was definitely achieved and the city of Buenos Aires was declared to be the capital of the republic and the seat of the national government.

Chapter III

LIFE AND WORKS

Domingo Faustino Sarmiento — a man possessed of a personality so great, so rich, so fruitful, so varied, so vivid that it is difficult to find words to describe him without running into an abundance of superlatives. Fame is his not only in his native Argentina, where he rose from the humblest of conditions to the position of the highest magistrate, the President of Argentina, but throughout South America he is known as the greatest educator of the continent. Having visited the United States twice, the first time on a brief educational mission, and twenty years later as Minister of Argentina, he became well known in the United States also.

Sarmiento has been compared to Lincoln and there is much similarity in these two great individuals. Both were born in poverty, in the interior of their separate continents; both were blessed with wonderful mothers; both were fired with an insatiable desire for learning and both surpassing seemingly indomitable obstacles, reached the highest position of trust in their respective countries and both saw their countries torn by internal strife but lived to see them united and on the road to greatness.

Sarmiento has been called Argentina's outstanding citizen and the true representative type of American in the same way that Voltaire and Victor Hugo represent France and Dostoevski and Tolstoy Russia.

Domingo Faustino Sarmiento is one of the most typically American personalities. He incarnates this continent as few others have. He emerges as the precursor of the New Man who is to develop in its land: a lover of liberty and of the rights of man, of tolerance and mutual responsibility. He was ever mindful of the unity of America, in anticipation of all

Courtesy the National Archives of Argentina

Mrs. Paula Albarracín Sarmiento, his mother.

mankind, so bitterly sundered and lacerated at the present time.[1]

Among the men which South America produced during the 19th century, Sarmiento, is without doubt, the outstanding one because he combines the intensity of his ideals, the abundance of his work together with the achievement of great influence. His temperment possesses the mystery of the indigenous together with Spanish tradition of his race. It is possible that he had a trace of Indian blood, but he attacked the natives for their backwardness. Nor was he European, for when he traveled to Europe, he sharply criticized Spain, France and Italy for their political backwardness and widespread misery.

The struggle between civilization and barbarity is realized in its soul: a conflict of nature and history, of tradition and progress. In Sarmiento, the Indian and the Spaniard coexist and fight.[2]

Throughout his life Sarmiento was a patriot, though not in a narrow sense, and a sincere believer in democracy. The grandeur of the American continent filled his soul with joy and fired his enthusiasm with regard for the New World. This lead him to be interested in all the problems of America and the imposing bulk of his 52 volumes is devoted almost entirely to America. For over a half a century he wrote tirelessly in his efforts to better the world.

If we believe him to be a man of genius it is because he brought a message and fulfilled his arduous undertaking with the constancy of an apostle and the faith of a missionary. He saw the South American reality with anguished clarity and tried to transform it abruptly, without any solidarity with the past, by means of new methods and in virtue of hopes that transcended the destiny of our Continent to the destiny of humanity. America has not produced another man like him, nor does Europe have in its history a personality that resembles him. He used journalism and the school in an illiterate country for a political intent and succeeded in attaining the social reform he proposed for himself. His originality consists in that.[3]

Sarmiento boasted of having been born nine months after the Revolution of the 25th of May as if he had been conceived in the joy of the holy ecstasy kindled by that historic event. His birth on the 15th of February 1811 is attested to in the following terms:

In the year of the Lord 1811 on the fifteenth of the month of February, in this main church of St. John of the Frontier and parish of St. Joseph, I, the assistant priest, gave oil and chrism to Faustino Valentín, one day old, legitimate son of don José Clemente Sarmiento and doña Paula Albarracín. The other priest, Friar Francisco Albarracín, baptised him. Godparents don José Tomás Albarracín and doña Paula Oro, whom I advised of their spiritual relationship, and so that it be confirmed, we signed it. — José María de Castro.

We can see by this birth record that his real name was not "Domingo Faustino" but rather "Faustino Valentín." However, his family called him by the name of their traditional saint and thus he came to use the name "Domingo."

Sarmiento describes his birthplace, San Juan, as "an ignorant and backward province." (III, 6) It was this and nothing more, a small village, poor and backward, situated at the foot of the Andes in the interior of Argentina. The customs were those of the Spanish Colonial period, very simple and the language of the conquerors had been preserved almost intact. However, San Juan was the theatre of heated struggles during the childhood of Sarmiento for it was here that the new ideas came in violent contact with those typically colonial. Sarmiento grew up in this period of transition and his mind was subjected to the double current of these contradictory influences. But he overcame both and became a harbinger of New Argentina.

Against this somewhat dismal picture, but casting on it a rosy light, is to be seen the exquisite silhouette of a rare and unusual woman, Sarmiento's mother. She was the daughter of a well known family, the Albarracíns, who had been founders of the colony of San Juan.

Crossing the Andes of the Cuyo region the Spaniards, who three centuries before had founded the colony of San Juan, had come from Chile. Sarmiento was descended from those colonizers, among them the Albarracíns, — maternal family name — of Arabic origin; but their descendants ceased to be Spaniards or Arabs and were assimilated into the Huarpe land.[5]

Sarmiento speaks further of his mother's people and traces his family back to the beginning:

Midway in the twelfth century a Saracen chief, Al Ben Razin, conquered and gave name to a city and a family that later became Christian. Monsieur Beauvais, the celebrated French sculptor, not knowing my maternal family name and without having seen me without a burnoose, caused me to notice that I had a completely Arab face; and as I remarked to him that the Albarracíns had, in spite of the family name, green or blue eyes. In Algiers the similarity of features of the Argentine gaucho and the Arab surprised me. (III, 45)

Describing his mother's family further he says candidly:

I have found the Albarracíns, nevertheless, bordering on the common bone pile (into which bones taken from the grave are thrown) of the dark and wretched masses. Besides that aunt, there was another of her brothers, an imbecile whom she supported; my Uncle Francisco earned his living curing horses, that is, practicing veterinary medicine unwittingly. Of the other eleven brothers and sisters of my mother, several of their children still wear the poncho, with their feet on the ground, earning a *real* and a half per day as day laborers.

And nevertheless, this family has occupied a distinguished place during the Spanish colony and from its bosom have come forth high and intelligent men who have honored letters in cloisters, the congressional tribunal, and (have) worn the tassels of Doctor (Ph.D.) or the bishop's miter. The Albarracíns are distinguished even among the common people by their green or blue eyes, as I mentioned before, and the prominent sharp nose that is not aquiline. It has the reputation of transmitting from one generation to another intellectual aptitudes that seem genetic, and that our four or five generations have produced Dominican monks, well

Courtesy the National Archives of Argentina

Sarmiento's birthplace and his mother's loom.

presented priests who end with Friar Justo de Santa María, bishop
of Cuyo. (III, 46)

However, illness had depleted the family's resources and
Sarmiento's mother's inheritance was little.

> The social position of my mother was sadly marked by the
> meager inheritance that had been handed down to her. Don
> Cornelio Albarracín, owner of half of the Zonda valley and of
> multitudes of wagons and mules, after twelve years illness left
> poverty to be divided among fifteen children and some plots
> of unpopulated land. (III, 129)

Being by nature an industrious young woman, Sarmiento's
mother, had worked tirelessly in weaving fine woolens for the
religious orders and had saved the money she earned to be used for
the construction of the home that was to house a new family.

In 1801 doña Paula Albarracín, Don Cornelio's daughter, a
young woman of twenty-three, was undertaking a higher

Courtesy the National Archives of Argentina

The fig tree at Sarmiento's birthplace in San Juan, Argentina.

work, not so much as to strength as to the idea of an unmarried young woman. There had been the previous year a great scarcity of serge, a material much used for the habit of the various religious orders, and from the production of her weaving my mother had collected a small sum of money. With it and with two slaves of her Irrazabal aunts, she began the foundations of the house she was to occupy in the world upon forming a new family. With those scarce materials that were few for such a costly work, under one of the fig trees she had inherited on her land, she established her weaving shop, and from there, the shuttle coming and going, helped the laborers and carpenters who were building the little house; and on Saturdays she would sell the cloth made during the week, paying the artisans with the fruit of her labor. (III, 130)

This was the home Sarmiento was reared in under the loving care of his family. It was from this home that he later had to flee to Chile and it was to this same home he returned many years later as Governor of San Juan. Today in San Juan there is a statue of Sarmiento, honoring their most illustrious son and not far away still stands the birthplace of Sarmiento, with a fig tree which replaces the one which long ago was cut down.

Sarmiento would have liked to prove himself descended from the explorer, Sarmiento de Gamboa, who founded a colony in the southernmost part of Argentina and for whom a peak has been named in the Strait of Magallanes, but he regretted that he could not prove this lineage. Of his father's family he writes:

In 1650 the name of doña Tránsito Sarmiento was found registered in the archives. From then on I lose trace of this family and the most laudable efforts on my part is to the Provincial Governor Sarmiento, founder of the Magellan Colony, of bitter memory, failed despite there being a tradition that the Sarmientos of San Juan were Basques like him. (III, 132)

Though his father was of an old established family, he was greatly criticized for having spoken so frankly of him in *Recuerdos de provincia*.

With these elements, the noble worker became associated in marriage, shortly after her house was finished, with don Jose Clemente Sarmiento, my father, a genteel young man from a family also decaying like hers, and she brought him as dowry the chain of privations and poverty in which she spent long years of her life. My father was a man endowed with a thousand good qualities that were detrimental, that worked in the opposite direction without being bad. Like my mother he had been reared in the rough work of the time, a laborer on the paternal ranch La Bebida, muleteer with the herd,

handsome of face and with an irresistible passion for the
pleasures of youth without that machine-like constancy that
founds fortunes. And with the new ideas that came with the
revolution he had an invincible hatred for the material, un-
intelligent, rough work in which it had been created.
Speaking of me, I once heard him say to the priest Father
Torres: "Oh no, my son will never take a plow in his hands!"
And the education he was giving me showed that this was a
fixed idea born of profoundly bitter reflections in his spirit.
In the bosom of poverty I was nurtured as a nobleman and
my hands did nothing more than my games and pastimes
required. . . .

With these antecedents my father spent his whole life in the
beginnings of speculations whose earnings were dissipated in
ill-advised moments. He worked with tenacity and would fall
into discouragement. He would make efforts again and would
run into some disenchantment, using his energy on long trips
to other provinces until I had reached manhood. From then
on he followed in camps, in exile or in emigrations, the
fortunes of his son like a guardian angel in order to set aside
if possible the dangers that could threaten him. (III, 130)

Sarmiento's father had been a soldier of the Army of the
Andes under San Martín and it was with pride that he spoke of his
father's part in the Independence.

My father is a good man who has no other notable thing in
his life than having lent some services in a subaltern job, in
the war of independence. He took part in the battle of Chacabuco and for his patriotic fervor his contemporaries gave him
the nickname of father of his country. (III, 4)

From these two distinctly different individuals, we can very
easily trace those characteristics of Sarmiento.

If Domingo did not resemble physically his forefathers,
morally his heritage was manifest: from his mother a
religiousness, esthetic delight, constancy in work, austerity in
poverty; from his father impressionable fantasy and the joy

of adventure. What there is of geniality in Sarmiento is his own: his exceptional talent, excessive sensitivity which marked him as crazy, and a rough personality forged in abnormal circumstances.[6]

Of the fifteen children which Sarmiento's parents, had, only five lived to reach maturity, being the sisters of Domingo, Paula, Bienvenida, Procesa and Rosario. Sarmiento's mother had little economic help from his father and with such a large family to provide for, she continued her weaving at the loom under the fig tree. The family became accustomed to being wakened at daybreak by the sound of the loom at which the tireless mother continued her labors for many years. She was truly a grand matriarch, a devout Christian whose deep faith was a solution to all the difficulties of her life.

In later years, Sarmiento tells of the fantastic beings who frequented his nights and such an authentic testimony shows us the rare spirit of this man.

When the light was turned out, my martyrdom began. A moment later when I was beginning to fall asleep, shapeless masses, a yard and a half tall like the pins in bowling, came out of every corner. They were animated beings without discernible faces and would begin a dance, whirling around the interior of the room. They did me no harm nor did they come toward my bed. I was in the dark, watching them in terror, not daring to scream for fear that they would become irritated, eat me up, who knows? And this lasted for years. Finally I became accustomed to these and other scenes; they were like my friends, my acquaintances. The light of day and refreshing sleep brought happiness and oblivion of the past terrors. Once I told my mother and sisters of these strange visions. Who pays attention to the foolishness of a child? And so I lived tranquilly with fantastic beings. (XLV, 277)

There remained in San Juan during his childhood Indians and mestizos and perhaps it is from them that Sarmiento heard tales of magic and believed in them. The superstitions that surrounded this archaic village even led to a belief in witchcraft until about 1830. All of this must have had an influence upon the sensitive Sarmiento. That he believed in a mysterious power beyond that which we can see is apparent from reading *The Life of Young Domingo*

> I believe in many and very mysterious tales that escape the well-known laws and which logic rejects. . . . As for me, I believe firmly that we are surrounded by an atmosphere of emanations which are sympathetic to those of our friends who sense our approach, with which our image and memory is awakened in their memory and are already awaiting us when we come. (XLV, 253-255)

Educational opportunities in San Juan during Sarmiento's childhood were few. However, he entered school at the age of five years where he learned to read very well.

> My father and the schoolmasters encouraged me from early childhood to read, for which I acquired some celebrity for then, and for later a decided fondness for reading, to which I owe the direction that my ideas were to take later. (III, 7)

There are three people important in the early training of Sarmiento, his mother, that unsurpassed model of motherhood, his first teacher, Don Ignacio Fermín Rodríguez, and his uncle, the curate Don José de Oro. His mother instilled in him a devout sense of duty, a love for work, perseverance in endeavor and a sense of the necessity for dignity, to meet the vicissitudes of life. Thanks to Rodríguez, the school became all important and this first classroom provided the original stimulus of his attitude of mystical exaltation toward education. Don José de Oro made a man of him in every respect, awakened in him a lofty sense of personal independence and taught him to be upright and valiant. His mother had entrusted his moral training to the uncle in the hope that Domingo might follow in his footsteps and become a priest. Sarmiento loved his uncle dearly and says of him:

> My intelligence was molded under the imprint of his and to him I owe the instincts for public life, my love of liberty and the fatherland, and my devotion to study of the things of my country from which neither poverty, nor exile, nor absences of long years could distract me. I left his hands with my

reason well formed at the age of fifteen. (III, 55)

Because of his superior talents, everyone hoped that he could continue his education. The school authorities nominated him for a scholarship in Buenos Aires but when the awards were made, his name was not among them. This was a severe blow to Sarmiento and he often lamented his lack of a formal education, but he was not discouraged. He learned Latin, French and English and read all the books he could find, books of philosophy, history, political theory and education. One of the books which he read was the biography of Franklin and this book had such an influence upon him that he felt that he, too, could someday make a place for himself in letters and American politics. Years later, he declared that the life of Franklin should be in every school library.

When he was fifteen years old, he began to teach at the side of his uncle, the priest Don José de Oro. Even though he was younger than his students, they recognized him as a man. Even his family granted him the authority as head of the house; he attributes this fact to his character and education.

From the early age of fifteen I have been the head of my family. Father, mother, sisters, servants, all has been subordinated to me, and this dislocation of natural relationships has exercised a fatal influence on my character. Never have I recognized any authority but my own. (III, 20)

Later he entered business as a clerk where he was able to read a great deal. His aunt was one of the many women in Sarmiento's life who aided him in his studies. For two years he worked and read and in the year 1827 he made his first trip out of the country. Shortly thereafter, he entered the army where he was able to maneuver a victory and being so animated at his success, he seems to forget the horror of the civil war which brought tragedy to so many. He became prisoner and his life was miraculously saved by the Commander José Santos Ramírez. During the time he was hidden, he spent his time studying French with a dictionary. The following year, 1831 Facundo Quiroga triumphed and Sarmiento and hundreds of other unitarians had to flee for their lives.

When he arrived in Chile, Sarmiento was entirely without means and his first thought of earning his bread was by teaching a primary school. He was a "progressive" educator, well liked by his pupils and their parents but unfortunately, the governor of the district did not approve of his advanced ideas of education.

But Sarmiento was a popular young man. We have a vivid picture of his youthful exile:

Away from school the reputation of the school teacher is extended; his frankness, intellectual curiosity and haughtiness were praised. He has a few grown up pupils, as at San Francisco del Monte, among them a few young ladies. The boy blends the lessons; he speaks to them of his flat country in San Juan, of his arrogance in confronting don Manuel Quiroga. The eloquence of the young man captivates them. The fire of youth burns in them and in him. That foreigner shakes up a bit the monotony of village life with his virile energy and the romanticism of age twenty. The sentimental girls sweeten the hours of the poor exile. There is one of both Biblical and lyrical name, belonging to a distinguished Chilean family, who catches the great man. The love epic flourishes. . . . And on July 18, 1832, their daughter Faustina is born in the Andes.[7]

In 1833 Sarmiento went to the port city of Valparaiso, where for a time he worked as clerk in a store. His zeal for learning continued and he spent half of his monthly pay for English lessons. Later, we find him working in the mines at Copiapo and Chanarcillo. Sometimes he would rise in the middle of the night to study English. He translated by candlelight the works of Sir Walter Scott. But such difficult work together with his economic hardships weakened his great organism and he contracted typhoid fever. In 1836, he returned to San Juan to recuperate his lost health. At the age of twenty-five, he already suffered political persecution, misery and exile.

Back in his native San Juan, he did not remain inactive but started learning Italian and at the same time decided to elevate the tone of the social life of his city. He wanted to polish the manners, cultivate the sense of humor and spread happiness in the theatre and dance. He decorated the local theatre and took part in the offerings. These pleasant events improved his health and made many friends for him. Nor was his love for the theatre or the dance a passing fancy because he always enjoyed them and stimulated them.

About 1838, together with Aberastain, Quiroga Rosas, Cortínez and Dionisio Rodríguez he founded a literary society. This gifted group of young men read philosophy and history and discussed the problems of the world. It was this period of his life that the influence of the French literature was great, and he became acquainted with Hugo, Dumas, Lamartine, Chateaubriand, Thiers, Guizot, Tocqueville and other French writers. Later Sarmiento wrote that he regretted that none of the gifted men had remained in San Juan, depriving the province of the benefits of the fruits of their intellects.

Already greatly interested in education, and believing that before a society could be genuinely enlightened its women as well as its men must be educated, Sarmiento founded the *Colegio de Pensionistas de Santa Rosa* which was inaugerated on the 9th of July of 1839. Here Sarmiento gave his first speech, one that was short and concise but nobly inspired. Naturally, such an event brought him great notice as there was no formal education for girls in all of Latin America at that time.

A secret love swayed Sarmiento's life at this time, but he did not declare his affection and the charming Clara Cortínez married another. He felt so poor, so weighted down with burdens that he felt he dared not reveal his love. But a half a century later, he revealed the silent love which had never been forgotten.

Shortly after the inaugeration of the girls' school, Sarmiento launched another enterprise, a newspaper, *El Zonda*, the first issue of which was published on the 20th of July 1839. All of this was much too advanced for the arbitrary and suspicious provincial authorities at San Juan and soon Sarmiento was in trouble again. Escaping death miraculously again, Sarmiento fled to Chile for another period of exile in November 1840. It was then that he wrote his famous sentence: One never kills ideas.

Back again in Chile, he at first thought of establishing a school in the city of Rancagua, of which he would be director and one of the teachers. Chile at that time was just as backward as Argentina, illiteracy was just as great and schools were just as scarce. However, before Sarmiento got his school established, an article he had written attracted the attention of the director of the Chilean newspaper, *El Mercurio*. Sarmiento was offered and accepted a place on the editorial staff. Later, he wrote for or edited several other Chilean papers. Through them he attacked Rosas and his dictatorial government in Argentina. It was during this period that he wrote his classic, *Facundo, civilización y barbarie*, which was a study of Facundo Quiroga, a semi-barbarous military *caudillo* of San Juan. *Facundo* was the first Argentine book to attract world attention; it was translated into French, Italian, German and English, and through it the *pampa*, the *gaucho*, Quiroga and Rosas acquired universal fame.

Sarmiento continued to maintain his interest in educational matters. His writings on education attracted so much attention that he was named on a commission by the national authorities of Chile to draw a plan for a normal school for the training of teachers. This was the second such school to be established in the Western Hemisphere, that of Horace Mann having been opened in 1841, two years before. In 1843, when the school opened, he was invited to become its first president. For two years Sarmiento taught several courses, wrote textbooks for use in the school and at the same time continued to write for the local press. It was not an unusual matter for Sarmiento to discharge the tasks of two or more full-time jobs.

Manuel Montt, an enlightened and progressive man, was the head of the educational system of Chile and he felt that the education of Chile's masses was necessary as one of the solutions of the country's problems. Even in remote Chile, news of the systems of primary education in Europe and the United States had reached Montt and he decided to send a commissioner to these foreign countries to learn what they were doing. Sarmiento was offered the commission. He accepted without hesitation and left Chile in 1845 and spent the greater part of the three successive years abroad — first in Europe, Spain, Italy, France, Germany and England and then in the United States.

When he was in London, Sarmiento read a book written two years earlier by Horace Mann, who had been in Europe on a commission similar to his. After he had read his book, Sarmiento was exceedingly eager to know this great educator. In Massachusetts the Chilean commissioner spent three days with Mr. and Mrs. Horace Mann. They were thrilling days for him, devoted to a deep discussion of educational matters with a master of such things. He had studied English but though he read it well, he was not fluent in speaking it so Mrs. Mann acted as his interpreter translating his French to her husband. Sarmiento was greatly impressed by the advance in education which our country enjoyed and it especially amazed him and delighted him that almost everyone could read, whether laborer or banker. Sarmiento traveled westward through the Central States and went down to New Orleans on an Ohio-Mississippi River steamer. While he observed certain crudities in our manners, he frankly liked our people, forming an opinion of them which many think was somewhat idealized.

Back in Chile, Sarmiento made his report which he published in 1848 under the title *Informes sobre educación*, which was a plea for education and schools for everyone. Though all the recommendations were not put into practice immediately, eventually they were incorporated in the school systems of both Chile and Argentina with the result that these two countries are the best organized and advanced of all South America.

A few months after his return, Sarmiento married the widow of the wealthy owner of the mines at Copiapo. He had known her for many years and her son, Domingouito Fidel, took the name of Sarmiento. In fact, Palcos declares that he was really Sarmiento's own son.

The only son of doña Benita, Dominguito Fidel — born in the Chilean capital April 25, 1845 — came to bear the name of Sarmiento, his real father.[8]

In 1849 Sarmiento published another of his best books, *Viajes*, about his travels to Europe, Africa and America. In the early 1850's he returned to Argentina, thinking that he might be able to help in the overthrowing of the dictator, Rosas, but when he saw no place for his activities, he returned to his foster-country, Chile.

In the meanwhile, his friend, Manuel Montt, had become president of Chile. He made Sarmiento director of primary education and entrusted to him the editing of a monthly periodical, *School Monitor*, which gave Sarmiento an opportunity to print and distribute widely his views on education. As director he was also able to effect some improvements in the educational field. He also wrote another book about education, *Educación común*. In 1850 his autobiographical book, *Recuerdos de provincia*, was published.

This together with *Facundo* and *Viajes*, published in the early part of his life, are the three works considered outstanding of the fifty-two volumes which Sarmiento wrote.

In all of the years of exile, Sarmiento had lost none of his love for his homeland and was always waiting for the time when he could return and have a part in building a better country. He himself writes: "I have never lost sight of my country, never have abandoned nor renounced the political cause to which I have belonged." (III, 22) government. Sarmiento had gone to join in the battle to overthrow the dictator but shortly hereafter found that he differed with Urquiza in his new policies and again returned to Chile. At the port in Buenos Aires to see him off was his friend, Mitre, and Sarmiento told him in a prophecy that strangely enough came true, that he would be the first president of the Republic but that he Sarmiento reserved the second presidency for himself.

Early in 1855, Sarmiento felt that he might return to his native land again so he closed up his business affairs in Chile and crossed the Andes again to Argentina. When he returned, nearly everyone in Argentina had taken a position on the question of centralism or federalism in the nation's government. All wondered what Sarmiento's stand would be. He had written earlier that when he was in the provinces, he was a Porteño but then when he was in Buenos Aires, he was a provincial. This attitude he was able to maintain for some time after he returned and he did not mix definitely in the centralist-federalist struggle. He rose above the division by saying that first of all he was an Argentine.

In 1857 Sarmiento became a representative in the Buenos Aires Senate and being reelected, he remained until 1861. In this new role, he presented many useful projects, participated in important debates and became known as an able and informed legislator.

In 1862, Sarmiento was made governor of his home province. Here he continued his projects of education and advancing his people, and his was one of the most progressive governments the province ever had.

So many were his accomplishments for bettering his country during this time, that it seems incredible that one man could have been responsible for all of them. He caused schools, hospitals and sanitariums to be established, roads to be built, cities to be planned, he reorganized the administration of justice in the province, he caused the making of a new election law designed to prevent fraud and produce a more democratic system. Many other excellent projects were a result of his interest in bettering his country. Once in the Senate, when he was trying to raise money for the extension of railroads and the senators protested that his figure was too high, he answered that it was nothing, that even ten times the amount asked would be small. Such was the amusement of the Senators that Sarmiento asked that the entire argument be contained in the record so that the future generations could see with what fools he had had to contend.

Then in 1864, Sarmiento was destined to return to the United States. This time he was to go as Minister of Argentina to the United States and he was especially happy over the instructions given him to make a report upon education in the United States. He later said that the reason for his appointment was the desire to get him out of the country to prevent his becoming a candidate for president in the next election. But whatever the motive was, Sarmiento accepted.

Enroute to the United States, Sarmiento stopped to attend an international conference of the Latin American countries. He did this without official sanction of President Mitre and this argument produced a heated exchange of letters between the two great men.

He did not reach the United States until May, 1865, one month after the death of President Lincoln. The news of the president's death caused him great sadness, for now both of the men whom he had said he loved most were no more, Horace Mann having died in 1857. Nevertheless, Sarmiento spent three very happy years in the United States, renewing friendships with Mrs. Mann and others he had known on his first trip. Sarmiento wrote another book about schools, *Las escuelas, base de la prosperidad y de la república en los. EE.UU.* While he was in the United States, he also wrote a life of Lincoln, founded a magazine, *Ambas Américas* to carry scientific information throughout South America. He attended national educational conventions and made public addresses. He was awarded the honorary degree of Doctor of Laws by the University of Michigan and this pleased him very much.

And then a most interesting thing happened. While still in the United States, Sarmiento had been elected president of Argentina.

Without knowing the results of the election, Sarmiento had started home and when his ship reached Rio de Janeiro, he learned the news that he was his country's president-elect.

His six years of presidency were from 1868 - 1874 and they were great years for Argentina. Education, immigration, industrial and agricultural development were his chief concerns. At his request, Mrs. Mann selected several young men and women to go to Argentina to staff schools. Sarmiento founded an astronomical observatory at Córdoba, the first such institution in the Southern Hemisphere.

The years from the presidency to his death in 1888 were by no means idle ones. He occupied for several years the post of director of schools and worked hard, but his accomplishments fell short of his desires. Money was lacking and many people did not have his vision of what education could mean to the future of Argentina. However, with everything else that he did, Sarmiento continued to write for the press. So voluminous are his writings, principally in the newspapers, that when collected they complete fifty-two volumes.

Sarmiento died in Asunción, Paraguay where he had gone to enjoy the warm climate. He will always be remembered as South America's greatest educator. He was truly a great man in many ways — in honor, honesty, in intellect and industry and in his immense desire to make his people and the world better.

Courtesy the National Archives of Argentina

Sarmiento's home in Asunción, Paraguay, where he died in 1888.

Chapter IV

TRAVELS THROUGH EUROPE AND AFRICA ENROUTE TO THE UNITED STATES

1. Santiago to Montevideo

Nothing could have been more important in the shaping of the personality of Sarmiento than his travels which were to take him as a special envoy from the Chilean government to the principal parts of Europe and North America to compile studies concerning education in these countries. It was thanks to the foresight of the Minister of Education of Chile, Manuel Montt, that his trip was made possible. Sarmiento had dreamed of going to Europe but such a trip was not easy in those days and had it not been for the circumstances produced in Chile with the publication of *Facundo*, who knows whether or not this event would have taken place.

We know of his desire to visit Europe from a letter of his friend, Antonio Aberastain, written on March 16, 1845 in which he answers one of Sarmiento written on the 22nd of February, 1845 asking for material concerning the life of Facundo Quiroga. Aberastain approved of his plans and said: "Both his plan to go to Europe and that of entering somewhat more into the Argentine revolution are to my liking and complete agreement." (XLV, 95-96) However, we do not know what the plan for going to Europe was.

With the publication of *Facundo*, Sarmiento became the object of attempts by Rosas to demand the Chilean government to silence him. Many of the newspapers which carried on opposition to the government of Rosas began to soften their attacks. In some circles, there was also talk depreciating Sarmiento and his literary works. Montt, who was confident of Sarmiento's ability, had encouraged the publication of the book. On the 5th of May, 1845,

El Progreso commenced to publish *Civilización y barbarie. Vida de Juan Facundo Quiroga.* Throughout May and June, day after day, the torrent of literary eloquence continued. Sarmiento had begun the fight to overthrow the tyranny. His book would be the torch to lead the way. Now, none could deny his talent or capacity.

Sarmiento had been writing articles against Rosas in the Chilean newspapers, *El Mercurio*, and *El Progreso*, for some time and had early in 1845 published *Aldao*, a short biography of the famous *caudillo* of Mendoza. This prepared the way for *Facundo* which was to become the most important book about Argentina. Sarmiento had thought of writing *Facundo* and had written his friends for information in February, 1845. However, he had no time to document his book and it was ready for publication in *El Progreso* almost at the same moment as had arrived don Baldomero García, the Ambassador of Rosas, who while coming on the pretext of arranging certain commercial questions and frontier problems, had actually come to protest against the Chilean government for the attacks of the Chilean press against the government of Rosas, and especially of those written by Sarmiento. It is not hard to imagine the disgust which García must have suffered reading the daily installments of *Facundo* along with the other humiliations suffered during his mission, which ended in failure early in 1846, when he resigned.[1] Nor is it hard to imagine the satisfaction Sarmiento must have felt, knowing that the personal emissary of Rosas was present to read the powerful chapters as they appeared day by day for over two months.

Facundo was published in book form on the 28th of July, 1845 and ten days later Sarmiento entered into one of his bitter polemics with Colonel Godoy who had been attacking him in *El Diario de Santiago*. Shortly thereafter, Godoy was brought to court, not for charges by Sarmiento but rather by the city of Santiago. Godoy was acquitted and paraded through the streets with groups of his followers to whom he threw money, shouting against Sarmiento and Montt. This provoked Sarmiento into resigning as a newspaper man and planning to leave Chile for Bolivia. However, we learn of the proposal of Montt that was happily accepted by Sarmiento in a letter written on the 9th of October, 1845 to Juan María Gutiérrez in Valparaiso:

> The first part of his dream is sanctioned: 'am going off to Europe, I am going, I am going . . . I have made this resolve after a short talk with Montt last night. This is the only sure

way left for me. I am offered facilities for this and for nothing else. Montt is a good friend. Last night he made me feel this. The interview was to request my continuing the editorial work; at my first refusal, deploring and disapproving it, he said let us not talk more of this, now let us think of you. What do you plan to do? Go off to Bolivia? Don't do such a thing; you are going to grow obscure, to lose ground. Not even for the expectation of returning to your country. In the present circumstances men who will shed blood are needed, and you must not waver in that and must continue commanding for the future. You should enter your country by sea, from Europe, to organize. Go away and travel around for a year. Count on the means to do so. If you wish to return to Chile, you will be here whatever you want. You are feared, but nobody has contempt for you.[2]

And thus it was that at the end of October, Sarmiento commenced his trip which would take him to Europe, Africa and North America.

He left Valparaiso in a sailing vessel, the *Enriqueta*, after having said farewell to his friend, Montt, full of confidence and enthusiasm for the new adventure. Officially, he carried the mission of the Chilean government and the corresponding letters of credentials but besides those, he knew he had another entree. He said to Montt: "Look, Montt, to enter Paris I am carrying two valuable recommendations, the credentials of your government and *Facundo*. I have much faith in this book."[3] He knew that his friend shared his sentiments about *Facundo*.

As Sarmiento set sail on this adventure, he must have had leisure moments to remember the drama that his life had been up to the moment of this most important incident in his life. He was aboard a sailing vessel of poor accomodations but he found the life a new experience and passed hours listening to the interesting tales of the few companions and the crew. He liked to watch the endless procession of waves and at night he watched the stars come into view. He must have meditated about his life, about his home, his mother whom he adored, his sisters, the early disappointment of his father when he failed to obtain the scholarships to study in Buenos Aires or Córdoba, his schooling with his uncle, the priest Oro, the time spent as a storekeeper with his aunt doña Ángela, and the narrow escape at the hands of some of Aldao's mob. He must have remembered his first trip across the Andes, and the later ones, when he again fled for his life. He must have remembered the days as a teacher in that mountain settlement and the idyl there which gave him his daughter, the days in Chile where he worked in many menial tasks, from that of a storekeeper to a miner, and his illness which took him back to his beloved San Juan, from where he would again have to leave his loved ones to flee for his life. He must have wondered at the challenge that his life presented. He was thirty-four years old, full of enthusiasm and eager to know the world.

He tells of the first days out when the winds seemed to play with their hopes for a quick trip and how they learned to accept the contrary winds with resignation, after having found out that their anger was to no avail in meeting the elements of nature. He enjoyed the beauties of the sunrise and the sunset, he was inspired by the endless formations of clouds, the wideness of the horizon, he watched the flight of the gulls, the unexpected appearance of whales and the pleasure of watching the towering waves break and disappear. He described long hours of looking but not seeing, of not thinking, of not feeling, of being completely paralyzed by the power of the beauty surrounding him. Then he tells of the unfortunate experience of losing one of the sailors who fell overboard in a storm and it was impossible to save him. For Sarmiento, it was an unusually tragic sight to think that the poor sailor lost his life in front of the islands of Chiloé, where his mother and family would never see him again. From then on, Sarmiento could not enjoy the sea without remembering his unfortunate companion and he was forever watching for his appearance among the waves or listening for his shouts in the crash of the waves and the whistle of the wind. Nor were the stars so beautiful for even in the dark of the night, he was always remembering the lost sailor, who haunted his dreams and robbed his hours of sleep. Nothing could so vividly show us the great sensitivity and feeling of this soul which is revealed in this tragic event.

In front of the islands of Chiloé, a violent wind took them off their course and they found themselves in front of a desert island, upon which the captain declared there was nothing more than wild hogs and savage dogs. Nevertheless, Sarmiento and some of his shipmates decided to explore the island and set out in a small boat. They calculated the distance very badly and only after eight hours of hard rowing did they arrive, armed with their pistols and a stiff drink of rum. It was already night and the point of arrival was lined with perpendicular rocks. After several shouts by the pilot in English, they were surprised with an answer. The four solitary male inhabitants of the island, Más-a-fuera, were afraid their visitors would leave and they urged them to stay, saying it had been so long since they had talked with anyone. These men were at one time sailors who had probably deserted their ships or because of some crime preferred to escape from the world. They lived on the island, which had been visited by Cook a hundred years before, and about which Daniel Defoe had written *Robinson Crusoe*. Here they lived, wearing the skins of the goats which had multiplied in great numbers since Cook had left the first ones, eating the produce of their garden and the plentiful fish and goats. Sarmiento was charmed to see the drama of these four men living on the island of that childhood classic. He describes the hospitable fire, the improvised furniture, the beds made of hundreds of goat skins. But he doubts that one can attain complete happiness there, away from the demands of society, saying:

> A part of our souls would dry up like one side of paralytics if we did not have someone on whom to exercise envy, jealousy, ambition, greed, and any other eminently social passion which, in the guise of egotism, God has put into our hearts. (V, 13)

Sarmiento and his companions spent the night, got up early the following morning to go hunting, and returned to the *Enriqueta* where the others were all ears to hear of the adventure. And there was another passenger for the youngest of the four refugees had begged to go aboard the ship to go to Montevideo, and thus there were three left on the island, Más-a-fuera.

The trip lasted almost two months and early in December, the *Enriqueta* approached the Río de la Plata, whose muddy water was so different from that of the ocean. It was the first time that Sarmiento had been near the river and it was the first time he had been so close to Buenos Aires, the city he had longed to know. We can imagine the emotion he must have felt entering the stream of the Río de la Plata, when at his side the captain pointed out the red color of its water saying: "That is the blood of those who were beheaded out there." The captain had pointed toward Buenos

Aires and Sarmiento describing the moment says: "I stood there mute, sad, pensive, humilitated by what was once my country, just like a son ashamed by his father's insult." (V, 24)

Sarmiento arrived to Montevideo early in December and there he would meet for the first time many who would be friends for life. He mentions his meeting with Vélez Sarsfield, whose friendship with Sarmiento is one of the lasting ones formed in Montevideo. Another was Bartolomé Mitre of whom Sarmiento said:

> poet by vocation, gaucho of the pampa, through punishment imposed upon his intellectual instincts; an artilleryman, no doubt, trying to find the shortest route to return to his country; of easy spirit, an always moderate temperament and an excellent friend. (V, 63)

Sarmiento could not have arrived at a more propitious time to Montevideo. The city was besieged by Rosas with Oribe in command of the troops, six hundred of which were Spanish, and Sarmiento tells of the cruelties of the executions as heard from the Cerro. The city defended by those of different races, English, French, Italians, Spanish, Basques and Argentines. He was admirably received by those others who had fled the tyranny of Rosas. Hardly had he arrived when the news spread and he was greeted by Argentines of every class. His *Facundo* had been published in *El Nacional* since the 3rd of October and even though there were differences of opinion as to *Facundo*, one thing was certain, Sarmiento was a source of much controversy. Alsina gave him some notes to make corrections in *Facundo* but Sarmiento paid no attention to his suggestions. The greatest blow was by Florencio Varela, who told Sarmiento that *Facundo* was of no value but recommended *Aldao* without knowing that it was also by Sarmiento. Later on, Varela changed his opinion of *Facundo* after talking with a French Admiral and several Europeans who have said that it is the only book in America which deserves to be mentioned. The day that Sarmiento left Montevideo, Varela went to see him and stayed all day, and regrets that he had failed to know him until his last day.

Another of the dramatic encounters of Sarmiento in Montevideo was with Echeverría, which was one of the greatest pleasures for Sarmiento. He describes Echeverría as a "as tame a man as he is an ardent and passionate poet." (V, 60) Sarmiento spent many hours conversing with him about Argentina and admired his thought and his works. Rojas points out that Sarmiento omitted from his sketch of Echeverría the fact that he had organized the *Asociación de Mayo* in 1837 and had taken part in the revolution of 1839 and because of its failure had had to flee to Montevideo and was therefore a man of action, whereas Sarmiento prefers to admire his ideas and his poems. Rojas also suggests that it may be that Sarmiento was jealous of Echeverría and influence he held over the younger generation and points out that the judgment of Sarmiento about both Varela and Echeverría who passed away before Caseros, was more generous after their death.[4]

Since the ship which was to take Sarmiento to Rio delayed its departure, Sarmiento had ample time to enjoy and know Montevideo. He spent many hours with the Argentines exiled there and had formed a very personal interpretation of the question of the siege, although he was not complicated in it. In his letter to Vicente F. López, written in Montevideo the 25th of January 1846, he gives a vivid description of the city and the situation in which the many foreigners of Montevideo forged together in the cause of liberty, formed a new stronghold. Sarmiento as an artist was charmed with the beauty of the city but more than that he saw in Montevideo the prelude of the triumph of the future cosmopolitan city.

> "Oh, Montevideo!" he exclaimed, "I salute you, regenerated Queen of the Plata [River]! Your future is assured; the fire of the tall grasses in the desert has already passed over your surface; the grass that will grow will be fresh and soft for everyone. Exile from my race, one day I shall come to seek beneath your walls, the complete state of man, which Spanish traditions deny me everywhere. (V, 37)

For Sarmiento the siege of Montevideo wasn't just a battle of Rosas with the Unitarians or of Argentina with the former province nor of Americanism against the European aggressor but rather a life struggle for the survival of the Spanish Colonial spirit against the new spirit of the immigrants consolidated in Montevideo with the native Americans, imbued with the new ideals of liberty. For Sarmiento, Montevideo offered the hope of what he had struggled for, and perhaps he dreamed of returning to make it his home. We know with what bitterness he had considered leaving

Chile for Bolivia and it is perhaps that he saw in Montevideo the place where he might exercise his capacity and full rights. On the other hand, Sarmiento left Montevideo after having lived there two months more convinced than ever of his own doctrine. He criticized Oribe, the government of the besieged city, the agents and admirals of Europe, the Argentines and the Uruguayans. He observed all and obtained an experience that would be useful to him when he returned to join Urquiza in his campaign against Rosas. It is perhaps not an overstatement to say that after Sarmiento had met the leaders of the Argentines who had fled from Argentina, he was confident in his ability to lead his country, once Rosas had fallen.

2. Rio de Janeiro

Rio de Janeiro! What an impression the boundless beauty of this city gave Sarmiento. Twenty days after his arrival from Montevideo, he wrote his friend, Miguel Pinero, another of the exiles in Chile his brilliant description of the city and its inhabitants. The morning he wrote he said:

> It is barely six o'clock in the morning, my dear friend, and I am already exhausted, undone, just as is our poor physique when it has ventured beyond the limits permitted to pleasures. (V, 63-64)

He described the exuberance of nature in Rio, the brilliance of the sun, the profusion of flowers and fragrances and the effects the tropical beauty had upon him, saying:

> And then when one's eyesight has cast itself over this combination of pictures, of luminous shadows and reflected light, it communicates to the senses the fatigue of the spirit, spent with the feeling of the sublime. (V, 63-64)

Nor is it difficult to imagine the beauty that so overwhelmed Sarmiento for his description is a masterpiece of expression that is rivaled only by the actual beauty that is Rio's. One of the powerful descriptions is of the mountain Corcovado, of which he said:

> immense fragment of granite that advances in such a

menacing way over the perpendicular line, as if the nucleus of
the mountain had tried to stick out its head amid the con-
vulsions of agony, to breathe free air, suffocated by the
masses of vegetation, grasses, bushes, trees, vines, piled high,
superimposed intricately and impenetrably, that cover it
from the base to four-fifths of its total elevation. (V, 70)

For Sarmiento who had known the mountains of San Juan and
Mendoza with their barren summits of rock, the verdant
mountains of Rio were overpowering in their luxuriousness.

Besides describing the city amid the clouds and the mountains
and the sea, Sarmiento describes the inhabitants of Rio with the
same penetrating perception. He speaks of the negro, his physical
aspect, his difficult life, his grief, his mystery and the problem of
slavery. Sarmiento notes the native gift of song which accompanies
the merciless work of the negroes, who sang of the day when they
would forget all their troubles, the day when they would no longer
have to work but would find their solace in death. Sarmiento
discussed the mulatto, analyzed his psychology and predicted that
the day would come when he would avenge the wrongs done his
mother and give to Brazil its national physiognomy because he is
intelligent, active, typical of his geographical and historical atmosphere, and gifted in many ways.

Sarmiento analyzed the government of the Empire of Brazil,
and doubted that anything would come of the republican attempts
of *gauchos* in Sao Paulo and Rio Grande del Sur. He discussed the
economy based upon sugar and coffee and the plans for South
American leadership. He went everyplace, seeing, asking questions,
fascinated with everything. He visited the Botanical Garden with
the German scientist, Mr. Koning, who told him that the plants in
Rio grown in all their splendor were the most luxuriant in all the
world and that he would see the same plants in Europe but pale
and poor in comparison.

Sarmiento says that it is well to carry letters of introduction,
not only for the purpose of knowing the persons to whom they
are directed but in order that they may open new doors to a
traveler. He had a letter for the physician of the Emperor, Dr.
Sigaud, and through him Sarmiento met Dr. Chavannes, a
promotor of the silk industry in which Sarmiento was interested,
and diplomats from other countries in Brazil. Once at a luncheon,
it happened that Sarmiento was seated between the Minister of

France and the Uruguayan *caudillo*, General Rivera, who spoke of so many foolish things that Sarmiento had to hide his laughter with his handkerchief. Rivera spoke of the queen doña María de la Gloria and said that he had been asked to marry her but that he hadn't wished to. So many things he said that Sarmiento spoke in French to the French Minister and they had a good time laughing about all the boasts of the *caudillo*, whom Sarmiento described as: "What a tiresome, insipid blockhead! What lies he told and what ridiculous boasting, what a nobody!" (V, 79) But to overcome this blot upon Montevideo, Sarmiento tells of knowing a Dr. Vilardebeau, an American physician, who was very simple and modest and who accompanied Sarmiento in his visits to the schools in Rio. He speaks of meeting Mármol in Rio and calls him a jewel and compares his poetry with that of Victor Hugo and Lamartine. Another pleasant meeting was with Rugendas, an artist whom he had known in Chile. Sarmiento describes him saying that: "Humboldt with his pen and Rugendas with his brush are the two Europeans who have described America most vividly." (V, 84) He tells of Rugendas' ability to capture in his paintings the differences of the various inhabitants of the South American countries where he lived and traveled for twenty years. Even in a picture of the siege of Montevideo which he gave to Sarmiento, you can distinguish the Argentines from the Uruguayans, not from any difference in dress but rather from the variations of the Spanish type in the different parts of America. The Emperor encouraged the fine arts but Sarmiento didn't think it worth his while to see the imitations of Europe when he was soon to see the originals, saying: "In the matter of fine arts and of monarchy I reserve my opinion in order to go to see them at their birthplace, for here their imitations seem to me grotesque and foolish parodies." (V, 77) Sarmiento had said that the Emperor was

> a young man, idiotic in the minds of his subjects, most devout and a saint in the minds of his confessor who rules him; very given to reading and according to the testimony of a distinguished personage, an excellent young man who does not lack intelligence, although his judgment is hindered by lack of brilliance and the poor ideas of a disorderly education. (V, 78)

It was Sarmiento's first visit to Rio de Janeiro. Little did he dream that twenty-two years later, he would again pass the beautiful city and be welcomed by the same Emperor but as the President of Argentina.

3. Paris

Sarmiento tells of his trip from Rio to Paris in a letter written shortly after his arrival, May 9, 1846 from Rouen, France. He had met Chilean friends in Rio who were en route to Europe but had preferred to go in a different ship saying that: "With twenty Chileans one always stays in Chile even though one is in Japan." (V, 88) He had elected to go in the packet boat *Rose*, which he described as much more luxurious than any boats he had known on the Pacific. Of the forty-five passengers, there was only one other, a young man of twenty-four years of age from Argentina, who spoke Spanish, the remaining passengers being Brazilians and Frenchmen. He describes the reserve among the passengers who select their companions for the voyage. He also delayed in making his friendships but found two who were not only good companions during his two month trip but were helpful to him in Paris. One of them was the Commander Massin, whom his friend Saint-George had recommended, and the other was a young man of rare appearance, M. Tandonnet, who had come from Buenos Aires and had known Rosas and approved of his policy. Sarmiento describes this young man with the long black beard, the only one in Buenos Aires, for such was not the vogue with Rosas. Massin was a French captain who was returning from Tahiti. He had also been sent by his government to the Straits of Magellan and knew well the problems of this disputed territory. Sarmiento found much to talk about with these two men and although he did not agree with Tandonnet in his ideas about Rosas, or in his ideas about Fourier, he found them charming companions who were to continue to serve him when he arrived to Paris.

The voyage was long but it seemed longer to Sarmiento because he was anxious to arrive. He was eager to know the France he had dreamed of. When at last the shores of France appeared on the horizon, his heart leaped with joy yet he felt humble before all that he was to know and wondered about his manners and how he would be received in Paris. He describes his arrival giving those details which point out his humanness:

The coasts of France were finally outlined on the distant
horizon. Everyone was greeting them with gaiety as I was,
feeling humbled and fearful at the idea of soon presenting
myself into the bosom of European society, lacking social
behavior and manners, careful not to let the awkwardness of
the provincial person show through, which nurtures so many
jests in Paris. My heart was pounding as we approached land
and my hands were thoughtlessly passing over the buttons on
my suit, tugging at my dress coat, feeling the knot of my tie,
straightening my shirt collar, just as when the inexperienced
suitor is going to appear before the ladies. (V, 99)

However his first impression was bad. When the ship docked at
Havre, it was besieged with guides who surrounded the travelers
like flies, trying to put their cards advertising the hotels for whom
they worked in the hands of the passengers and even in their
pockets. Sarmiento avers that he has not been able to lose this first
impression saying:

Eh, Europe! sad mixture of grandeur and abjection, of
knowledge and stupidity at the same time, sublime and filthy
receptacle of all that elevates or degrades man, kings and
lackeys, monuments and pesthouses, opulence and uncivilized life! (V, 99)

Nor did he like Havre, which didn't seem to him to be a part of
France because of its modern buildings and its lack of landmarks.
On the other hand, he noted the colossal size of the American
ships unloading cotton and beautiful surrounding countryside. In
the trip down the Seine he was charmed with the landscape, the
green hills, the many ships on the river, the roving musicians, and
the glimpse of the belfries in the distance. There was so much to
see that he found that the boat moved too quickly for his eyes to
see everything and tells how he looked at first the left and then
the right and then behind to be sure he hadn't missed anything.
When we remember his deep interest in history and his studies, we
are not surprised that he was pleased with the many Gothic ruins,
the old abbeys, the castles and the reminders of the secular life of
France. He says that the best way to enter France is at the Havre
for then one passes all the historic past, the Normans and the
English, the traditions and battlegrounds of the middle ages with

their convents and their castles, and arriving at Rouen, the most notable collection of Gothic ruins to be found in any city of Europe. His artistic soul was touched with the city of Rouen, which he says is of the fifteenth century. He was overwhelmed with the cathedral and climbed the towers to touch them with his own hands being convinced that such works of art were products of human hands. His description of the cathedral is another of the masterpieces of Sarmiento and he tries to give the sensation of the Gothic artistry, the vivid colors of the stained glass windows, the architectural beauty along with the spiritual inspiration which he feels. And so it was that Sarmiento arrived at Paris, with the mixed emotions of joy and wonder.

Paris at that time was not the city which was to be a generation later, but even then it possessed prestige throughout the world and a mysterious charm which conquered one and all. Literature, science and art flourished. Woman was queen everywhere and along with her, the fine arts. Gaiety, cordiality and culture vied to give Paris its especial charm. Sarmiento who had known but a few of the American cities, was overcome with the dazzling city and it seemed to him marvelous that he should have arrived there.

Sarmiento describes Paris in a letter written September 4, 1846 to his friend Aberastain, found in *Viajes* pp. 114 - 147. Along with this we have information concerning his studies of the silk industry and his interview with General San Martín in Volume XLIX, p. 17 and his lecture to the French Institute of History in Volume XXI, p. 19. These are excellent sources to discover the young traveler's impressions. While it is true that he was charmed with Paris, he did not lose his sense of judgment. He was able to vary his opinions according to what he felt and thus it was that he praised, admired, studied, criticized or disputed about all he saw. That which he most admired was the cordial courtesy of the Parisians with the foreigner, the charm of the women and the mysterious something that was in the air of this charming city.

He began to feel himself Parisian as he wandered about the city, and that was his greatest delight. He found everything that a scholar could wish for, museums containing the history of the world, collections of plants, expositions of paintings, books by the thousands and all the political systems imaginable. He did not think that luxury corrupted the moral forces or that pleasure was enervating and found his proof in the Frenchman whom he described as:

> the most audacious warrior, the most ardent poet, the most
> profound scholar, the most frivolous man of elegance, the
> most zealous citizen, the young man most given to pleasures,
> the most delicate artist and the smoothest man in his dealings
> with others. (V, 142)

He declares that he has neither the time nor the money for such
pleasures but that he would put a brilliant page in his memoirs if
he had forty thousand francs to spend.

In spite of his wanderings about Paris and his good times,
Sarmiento found time to study and took a course about the silk-
worm. For this he had to go to one of the suburbs, Mainville.
There he knew Jules Belin, the son of one of the most important
printers in Paris, whom he would invite to come to Chile and
whom he would one day have as a son-in-law.

In his letter about Paris, a great part is devoted to the political
situation with Rosas and the Río de la Plata question. Sarmiento
met the most famous leaders and gives sketches of Berryer, Odilon
Barrot, Arago, Cormenin, Lamartine, Emile Girardin, Thiers,
Guizot and many others. Sarmiento was unable to make anyone
understand the real situation of his country or the reasons for the
civil wars or the barbarism of Rosas.

When he had said farewell to Montt, he had hoped that his
book *Facundo* would help him to become known in Paris but
although he had had the manuscript translated to French, he still
could not get it in the hands of one who would publish it. Finally,
after waiting for two months, he met the editor of the famous
magazine, *Revue des Deux Mondes*, who promises to publish it
within two months. But Sarmiento was not in France when it was
published. He had left Paris for Spain.

Sarmiento left Paris after having lost his illusions that France
could serve as a political model or as support against the overthrow of Rosas. He had been able to know many of the political
leaders and he was disgusted with them saying, "In this society
where I was always received with more distinction than I could
hope for, I have been able to put my hand deep into the present
wounds of France." (V, 141) In another powerful judgment, he
said: "a golden urn filled with dirty waters." (V, 126)

One of the high spots in Sarmiento's stay in Paris was his meeting with General San Martín, who, after securing the independence of Argentina and other South American countries, had chosen to live in exile rather than partake of the civil struggles in establishing the government in his country, Argentina. Sarmiento carried letters of introduction from Las Heras and other old friends. San Martín knew of Sarmiento's first article about him in Chile and received the young man with cordiality. Sarmiento says that he passed with San Martín "sublime moments which will forever be engraved on his spirit." (V, 137) All went well until the name of Rosas was mentioned and then Sarmiento experienced another disillusion. San Martín did not understand the internal policy of Rosas but was in favor of him because of his defense of the country against the foreign imperialisms. Sarmiento attributes San Martín's point of view to the fact that he was old and had been away from the country for so long that he was unable to understand the situation.

Sarmiento sensed the coming of the Revolution of 1848 in that he predicted the downfall of the political systems then in vogue. He wrote:

> I was present, then, without knowing it, at the final day of a world that was departing and could see the systems and principles, men and things that soon would yield their places to one of those great syntheses which cause the energy and moral feeling of man to burst forth after being squeezed by the pressure of forces, preoccupations and interests, tending toward levelling their institutions to the very height at which the knowledge that they have rights and justice has reached. (V, 4)

4. Spain

Sarmiento reached Spain in November 1846, having traveled by stage-coach from France. In his letter to his friend Victorino Lastarria, dated the 15th of November from Madrid, he gives a bird's eye view of Spain as he had seen it intellectually, industrially and politically. However, we must remember that Sarmiento had judged Spain before he arrived there and had stated his purpose as that of rendering judgment before the tribunal of America. He stated that he would do so severely and impartially.

Of the first, we can be certain, since he had been condemning Spain for all the problems of the struggling South American countries since 1841, and even blamed Spain for the fact that he was in exile. As for his impartiality, we find that the critics Ricardo Rojas and Manuel Gálvez, who were seldom in agreement, each agree that although Sarmiento pointed out many truths about Spain, he had followed his preconceived judgment. Rojas says:

> Its casual truths withstand very little scientific analysis, because they belong to the subjective world of the prophetic and spiritual. There is much he is unaware of, despite his having read so much, and there is much he omits or deforms because he is a militant thinker, polemic writer, apostolic preacher of a message.[5]

Gálvez says: "His former passion prevents him from comprehending Spain. If he had looked upon it with serenity, he would have seen in it an immense reserve of strength."[6]

Sarmiento spent almost two months in Spain, the most of which was spent in Madrid. We know that he wanted to know the soul of Spain and we know that he considered himself Spanish, still it is impossible to draw adequate conclusions from such a short visit. He experienced great emotion upon coming into contact with the traditions and the life of the Spanish people but he found little to his liking.

One of the moments when he was at peace with his mother-country was when he visited the Cathedral of Burgos. There on a moonlight night, he explored the ruins of the Cathedral and the ruins of the dwelling of the Cid. He and his companions saw the iron bar showing the length of the Cid's arms and concluded that he must have been a powerful and robust man, since none of them could match him. He says that he has never before experienced such a deep emotion as on this excursion and we feel that he and the Cid would have understood each other. He says:

> Burgos by night is the old Burgos of Castillian traditions, the home of the Cid, the most beautiful Gothic cathedral that is known. By day it is a poor heap of living ruins inhabited by a people whose aspect is all that one could wish, except poetic,

not even cultured, two ways of being that complement each other. (V, 156-157)

In Madrid, he admired the beauty of the Street Alcalá, which he called the brain of Madrid and one of the most spacious of Europe, and the Puerta del Sol, which he called the heart of Madrid, where he watched the people manifest their joys and their sorrows in a manner such as he had not seen before. He was brilliant in his scintillating description of the bull fights and even though he admits the human fascination for the cruelty displayed, he laments that such a people would not be able to conceive of progress as is manifest in railroads, industrialization or constitutional debates. Even though he condemns this sport as cruel and barbaric, he says that it is not as bad as drunkenness, which is the pleasure of the northern peoples, and points out that the Spaniard is a sober person, a fact proven by the cape he wears.

But Sarmiento was disgusted with many things. He first noted the drivers of the stage-coach, their dress and their cursing. He didn't like the beggars everywhere, nor the poems they used in begging. He noticed the patched clothing and the patches of different colors made him think that the people lacked a spiritual unity. The variety of costumes also added to this belief and he said that the Spanish provinces were each separate small nations and not parts of one nation. He says: "The man from Barcelona says: I am a Catalonian, when one asks him if he is a Spaniard; and the Basques call Castillians those they wish to designate as enemies of their race and jurisdiction." (V, 161) He considered the Spaniard as over-proud because of his disdain of foreigners and says that he accepts only the French and English.

For Sarmiento, the only progress evident is in Madrid. The rest of Spain is stagnant. There was no national navy, no roads, no common schools, no printing to speak of, as even the stamps and the engravings sold were printed in Paris. There were no hotels to speak of, or rather they were in the same condition as Cervantes described them. Nor did he find the theatre up to his expectations. He wrote to his old friend, Saturnino M. de Laspiur, on the 20th of November 1846, that during the festivities for the wedding of Isabel II, he had seen the play, *El desdén con el desdén*, but that it didn't give him the pleasure that it had when recited by him on one of the trips mule-back across the Andes in 1827.[7] In another instance he was very critical of the theatre and says: "I tell the truth, a vaudeville performance causes me greater sensations than all the Spanish repertory, ancient and modern." (V, 177)

Sarmiento analyzed his observations and placed them in certain epochs, pointing out that from primitive times the use of the broom without a handle was known whereas the broomstick is a modern invention, but there in Spain the broomhandle was still unknown, necessitating the back-breaking task of bending over in order to clean the floor. He noted that the plow used was the same wooden one used by the Romans and that the mules still used the same bells that jingle as the animal walks; likewise the oil lamps dated from the days when Spain was a colony of Rome. Several customs he noted from the times of the Arabs, such as the women's wearing of the veil, the oriental manner of sitting upon a rug in church, the industry of weaving matting and the influence of the Moors in the men's dress. The lack of interest in natural science, geology and Greek, Sarmiento attributes to the lasting influence of the Inquisition.

Sarmiento visited the land of Don Quixote, La Mancha and later Córdoba, the home of Seneca, and later Seville. Then passing down the river Guadalquivir, he arrived at Cádiz and from there to Gibraltar and later to Valencia and finally to Barcelona, where he terminated his visit to Spain. In Barcelona, he found much to please him and he praised the European aspect of the city, its active population and its industry. Here he found so much progress that he felt that he was no longer in Spain. In Barcelona, Sarmiento met Cobden and the two passed almost the whole night talking.

Sarmiento's judgment of Spain has been called severe. It is true that at the time Sarmiento visited Spain it was in a state of general decadence, with her old culture undermined, her people in ignorance and misery and her place in the world was of little consequence. The critic Ricardo Rojas gives Sarmiento the credit of having had the courage to speak as he thought. He says:

> The picture is horrible but truthful, and in that one must render justice to Sarmiento, because the great South American found that he needed to see Spain and he went to see it, and because he had the frankness to say what he thought. Just as he spoke about his Argentine fatherland, as he spoke of Chile and all America, and it should not surprise us in speaking of Spain he should be cruel through love. Much of

what he says could be rectified or refuted, but generally in his writing the picture is true. That decadence lasted until the so-called generation of '98, in which Unamuno and Joaquín Costa said the same as Sarmiento a half century before, and with the same anguished, furious tone.[8]

5. Africa

While Sarmiento was in Barcelona, he met the famous engineer, M. Ferdinand de Lesseps and the great French writer, Prospero Mérimée. But he was most impressed with Cobden, the famous British free trader, whose economic ideas and manner of action were so similar to his. Before he left for Africa, he had the pleasure of seeing his *Facundo* reviewed in the Parisian magazine, *Revue des Deux Mondes*. There is no doubt that to have finally received this notice from Paris was an event which brought great satisfaction to Sarmiento. In the early part of December, Sarmiento left for Argel by way of Mallorca. In a letter to his friend, Juan Thompson, whom he had met in Barcelona, dated the 2nd of January, 1847, he tells of his voyage and his impressions of Africa. We know that Sarmiento was a good traveler but never had he been called upon to travel in such circumstances as befell him in his three day voyage from Mallorca to Argel. He had bought passage and because he was bored he went even when he saw the boat he was to travel in. It was a sailing vessel of about thirty feet with no accommodations of any kind. He was passenger along with three women, four sailors, thirty pigs, two dogs, several dozen of chickens and turkeys along with the barrels, bundles and other freight. With only his cape to protect him from the cold December weather, the wind, the rain and the hail, he bravely suffered the three long days and nights. He tells of his modest companions who sensed that he was an important person and favored him with every attention. But finally at the end of the third night they entered the bay of Argel. We know that his visit to Africa had been a part of his plan ever since he left Chile. He wanted to see the desert and the Arabs because he had imagined that they were similar to the Argentine *pampa* and the *gauchos*. He was happy to leave this uncomfortable sailing boat and he was overcome with emotion when he saw the white houses of Argel stretched out before him. Upon entering the city his emotion was even greater. He saw the magnificent hotels, the perfume shops, the bars, the art galleries, the walls covered with advertisements, the hundreds of carriages and the city full of movement and life. He saw the different races that made up the population, the Moors, the Arabs, the Jews, the Turks, each with their characteristic costume, and also the French, Italians and the Spaniards. He himself says that he forgot all the trials and tribulations of his terrible trip in the excitement of seeing for the first time this city of the Orient.

He describes the city, its motley people, the women, the Arab and his religion, his organization, the Koran and the historical antecedents of the Semitic peoples. He visited the outskirts of the city and saw the rows of shops whose owners sat in the door, weaving, smoking or sleepy and silent. He had brought a letter of introduction from de Lesseps to the Marshal Bugeaud, the French military governor of Argel and he discussed the similarity of the systems of fighting that exist in the desert and in Argentina. From Argel, Sarmiento went to Oran.

The ship made its last stop in Mers-El-Kebir, and there the passengers went to Oran in stage-coach along a highway carved out of rock between the sea and the mountains. Sarmiento carried a letter of introduction from Bugeaud to the General there but in his absence, he was greeted by the local Arab chief who offered him horses and a guide to visit a tribe. Sarmiento, dressed in a burnoose, accompanied by an interpreter and a Turkish official, set out on their Arab steeds. This visit to an Arab village is one of the most amusing of Sarmiento's travels. He had complained of the food in Spain but never before had he been called upon to partake of such a banquet as was given him on this tribal visit. He as guest of honor had to begin the feast. He says that he ate everything as if he had never had any fear for any dish and describes the cold sweat that ran down his body as he swallowed the *cuscussu*, a dish made of flour without salt and served in milk.

Sarmiento tells of seeing a group of women who immediately covered their faces with their veils when he approached. He wanted to see them and decided to try his skill. He pretended to not notice them anymore. Then suddenly, he seemed to find something in his path. He stopped, kicked at it, turned the supposed object over, and the women who had been approaching, were overcome with curiosity and dropped their veils. At this moment, Sarmiento turned around and saw the Arabian beauties with "beautiful eyes, eyelashes joined together by blue tattoo

marks and cheeks dyed as bright a rouge as the color of an apple."
(V, 228) Then he knew that women are the same everywhere,
always curious. And he adds that is all that he was able to see of
the charm of the Arabian women. But with such successful
strategy, he should have gone further.

Returning from a hunt one day to the house of General
Arnault, Sarmiento was feted by the high officers and before
dinner, he was pleased to be shown a copy of the *Revue des Deux
Mondes* which contained the review of his *Facundo*. Naturally, he
was pleased when the General said: "See how even now in the
center of Africa we are informed about what is happening in the
world" pointing out the title, *Civilización i barbarie. (V, 233)*
Later they discussed the similar customs of the Arabs and the
gauchos in smelling the earth or eating grass in order to find their
bearings.

As he remembered his native Argentine, he wondered why the
extense rich land could not be populated. He asked his friend Juan
Thompson why the current of emigrants that was going from
Europe to North America could not be diverted to South America
so that new cities could fill the space from the Plata to the Andes.
Thus we see that Sarmiento had his country ever present in his
mind.

6. Italy

As Sarmiento ended his letter to his friend Juan Thompson
about his experiences in Africa, he said:

In Rome there is a Pope, who dries the tears of his people; in
Venice the unburied corpse of a republic, and in Naples the
crater of Vesuvius and the mummies of Herculaneum and
Pompeii which I want to see at close range. (V, 239)

With such a program in mind, he landed at Civitavecchia on the
morning of the 8th of February, 1847.

His first impression of the people was not favorable and he
says that they abused the tourists in every way to obtain money
from them. His description might remind us of present day
traveling in South America.

But what most attracts the attention of the traveler in Civitavecchia are the marvelous inventions of the inhabitants to take possession of the money of sojourners, a most abundant trade as Lent approaches: a coin for disembarking a person and another for each piece of baggage; still more to carry this to the customhouse; one coin to move them, another to put lead seals on them; one coin for those at the gate; one coin to put them in the stagecoach; and if the traveler wishes to give anything to the porter, the coachman, the beggar, the clerk, the women, the children, and even the buildings if only they could hold out their hands! (V, 243)

On the road to Rome, he was impressed with the poverty of Italy. Not only were there beggars everywhere but the people along the countryside were dressed in skins of animals, which reminded him of the fauns and satyrs of mythology. The land was poor, without trees and muddy where there were no hills, but for which he might have thought he was in the *pampa*. As darkness arrived, an accident befell the stagecoach, perhaps, Sarmiento says because of a quarrel with the driver about the demands for money from everyone. At any rate, the stage coach crashed against a stone pillar on a bridge and lost a wheel. Fortunately, the passengers were only frightened and were able to obtain passage in another vehicle, excepting Sarmiento and a French missionary who continued the trip walking since there was not sufficient space for all. He tells of the lonely road and the fears that beset one when he is tired and in strange surroundings. Finally, they reached Rome and the same extortions for money were repeated. Even the sentinel had his hand outstretched. "Oh, descendants of a regal race, how unworthy of your ancestors you prove to be!" (V, 244)

It was five o'clock in the morning and Sarmiento tired though he was, says that the best way to overcome fatigue is curiosity. So without even resting, with the sun rising over the hills of Rome, he went to see the sights of the city he had dreamed of. It was with deep emotion that he saw the many points of interest of the city he had studied in his youth. Then he returned to his lodging, where almost all the guests were priests or their friends. Here he followed the religious customs and remembered his boyhood days when he was an altar boy for his uncle. He describes his visit to Rome and the surrounding points in a long letter to the uncle, who was then Bishop of San Juan, in his letter from Rome, dated the 6th of April, 1847.

He describes the city, its monuments, its temples and works of art in excellent terms. He speaks of the ancient aqueducts as reminding him of the backbone of some monster of antediluvian times. He had arrived the day that Carnival began and his descriptions of this celebration which came down from the old celebration of Saturn are among the best pages of his writings.

A large part of the letter concerns Sarmiento's visit to the Pope. Pius IX had recently become Pope after the dramatic years under Gregory XVI. Sarmiento tells of the jubilant people who received the new Pope and his liberal policy of opening the doors to those exiled, freeing the political prisoners and many other measures that filled the hearts of the people with hope. The Pope had visited South America in 1823 and asked Sarmiento questions about those he had known then and about the present government.

Sarmiento left Rome for a few days in order to visit Naples, Pompeii and Vesuvius. He writes his uncle of his early reading about the ruins of Pompeii and surely the good Bishop must have been pleased to hear from his nephew of the delight at seeing the ruins which he had taught him about. Sarmiento was charmed with Pompeii and the ruins and says:

> Finding these ruins has better served the undersnding of history than all the books and Roman monuments, for the distribution of the inhabitants, the utensils found, the announcements and posters written on the walls announcing performances and spectacles; in short, the multitude of bronzes, frescoes and adornments have made one guess at the pleasures, occupations, ideas and manner of being of the men who lived in those cities. (V, 287)

At Vesuvius he speaks of the joy of experiencing great fear. He had climbed to the summit of the volcano and saw what neither Dante nor Virgil saw. And like a child, he was incrusting money in the warm lava when suddenly there came a downpour of rocks. It was another of the narrow escapes in his life. He tells of lowering his head and rounding his shoulders as a huge rock fell only a few feet from him.

Sarmiento returned to Rome for Holy Week. He speaks of the grand ceremonies and the many protestant tourists who were present. He says that the ceremonies were worth seeing but that they were not as religious or as solemn as the ones in his province, San Juan, which he describes with a nostalgic tenderness as he remembers the full moon covering the populace as it filled the street and plaza to pray.

From Rome, Sarmiento went north to visit Florence, Venice and Milan. The impressions of this visit are described in his letter to his friend, J. M. Gutiérrez, dated the 6th of May 1847, from Milan. Sarmiento was very much impressed with the beauty of northern Italy and compared it to a delightful garden, saying: "The Appenines are gradually disappearing and let one see an immense land, a boundless plain, planted with cities, villas and covered with trees and verdure." (V, 312) And then he remembers the *pampa* of Argentina, which he had never seen but had described by hearing about it from the mule drivers of San Juan, the soldiers of the civil wars and the poems of Echeverría, and wonders why it can't be a garden instead of a wilderness. He answers by saying:

> ... because the people of Buenos Aires with all their advantages are the most barbarous that exist in America: rude shepherds, in the manner of the Kalmucks (of Mongolia), have not yet taken possession of the land; in the pampa one must complete the work of God through skill. The canvas being given, one needs the palette and paints that will color it. (V, 312)

No matter where Sarmiento was, he was forever dreaming of his Argentina and selecting the best of whatever he saw with the hope of transplanting it to his native soil.

Besides the natural beauty of the landscape, Sarmiento was overcome by the artistic grandeur which he found everywhere and was deeply moved by the treasures of the past, the many paintings, the mosaics and especially the statues. He said that the city of Florence seemed like a museum where all the artistic glories of the past were assembled. He saw the wonderful libraries, with their many works, some of them original manuscripts dating from the time of the Romans.

In the stage coach from Rome Sarmiento had met a young Frenchman, born of noble rank, who had become a republican much to the disgust of his family and friends. He and Sarmiento traveled together and were good companions until their paths separated. They stayed together in Venice and were able to pulse the sadness of this city under the rule of Austria. Sarmiento tells of the books he and his companions, Emilio and Champgobert, read with great interest, Lamartines's *Jirondinos*, Michelet's *Republic*, Gioberti's *Del primato degli Italiani* and another by Luis Blanc. These works were prohibited in Austria and thanks to the daring of Sarmiento entered Venice with him and Champgobert and Emilio. A gondolero who had been a friend of Emilio's family told them first hand of the tyranny under which Venice was living, ruled by Austria.

Sarmiento left Italy fatigued with having seen so much. He criticizes his lack of appreciation but it wasn't that, for he did possess a great sensibility to the arts, but rather that he was satiated with seeing thousands of paintings, statues and monuments of the past. He feared that the excess of the past glories dominates the present and annuls the possibility of progress. As he left Italy he said:

> The eyesight is finally dimmed in the midst of such marvels, these Italian fine arts lavished everywhere on thousands of objects and which, nevertheless, are not bound to anything, are tiring. Eternal remains of past glories, they cast their shadows over towns that do not even have their own life or political existence. Its very memories kill Italy. (V, 321)

7. Sarmiento Leaves Europe

In his letter dated the 5th of June, 1847, at Göttingen, Sarmiento describes his travels in Switzerland, Austria and Germany. This letter was directed to his friend and protector, Manuel Montt, and extracts of the letter concerning colonization were first published in the *El Comercio* of Valparaiso while the entire letter was later included in *Viajes* pp. 321-344.

When Sarmiento arrived in Switzerland and compared it with Italy, he was overcome with the natural beauties everywhere. He described his feelings as follows:

> Switzerland is in natural beauties what Italy is in the arts;

here God directly, there the genius of man, enrapture the
spirit, elevate it and shake it with emotions renewed at every
step. But in Switzerland, as does not occur in Italy, one feels
a pleasant sensation of life, an intimate pleasure which
imprints a continual smile on the face. (V, 326)

His descriptions of the mountains with their perpetual snow,
the many rivers with their cascades, the forests of pine trees with
the farm houses neatly nestled on the mountain side, are among
the most picturesque. He was not only impressed with the landscape of Switzerland but also with the industrious population, the
local industries and the excellent communication over the
mountains. He spoke of the stage coaches traveling along safe
roads with good bridges and strong snow fences to protect the
traveler from avalanches and then the ever-present sleigh traveling
up and down the mountains transporting passengers or freight. He
found that even in winter, distance was no problem in the Alps
and remembered how different were the Andes. Above all, he
admired the Swiss people because of their love for work, liberty
and honor. He remembered his sadness and disappointment at the
sad state of misery and backwardness of most of the countries he
had visited. His indictment of them is severe.

In Spain there was in both Castilles (Old and New) and La
Mancha a people (who were) ferocious, ragged and hardened
in ignorance and idleness: the Arabs in Africa would have
turned me into a fanatic to the point of ruin, and the Italians
in Naples showing me the ultimate degree below zero to
which human dignity can descend. What do the monuments
to genius in Italy matter, if, looking away from them the eyes
fall upon a beggar people who hold out their hands and do
not remember the name of the Madonna, except looking to
show the depth of the wretched poverty of body and soul in
which it wallows! However, Switzerland has rehabilitated me
for the love and respect of the people, placing a blessing upon
it, although humble and poor, the republic which knows so
well how to impart dignity to man. (V, 327)

Not all of his impressions of Switzerland were good, for he saw
the democratic spirit as narrow as the valleys and the local
patriotism creating nationalism. He saw the different cantons

divided not only by physical barriers but also by differences in language and religion. But he admired the republic, its energetic inhabitants and even the classic struggle between the only means of unification, the two major parties, the conservatives and the liberals.

However, in the final count, Switzerland was winner by far in the judgment that Sarmiento weighed out to the countries visited. Sarmiento had his own yardstick for measuring the culture of a country, but even so, Switzerland distinguished itself.

> For me the greatest number of known truths constitutes only the certainty of an epoch, but only the most extensive appropriation of all the products of the earth, the use of all intelligent powers and all material forces, for the comfort, pleasure and moral uplifting of the greatest number of individuals, can characterize the civilization of a people. The same arms that cultivate the soil in Switzerland, manufacture watches and silk cloth; each house possesses an industry and each town ejects the column of smoke from its factory into the air. The isolated little Swiss house has no rival in Europe. (V, 327)

From Switzerland, Sarmiento crossed the border to visit Germany, as yet not unified. He was charmed with the gay city of Munich and the young couples dancing the waltz and the new dance, the polka. He lamented the fact that ideas don't spread as quickly as the dance but was glad for the happiness that the poor people can have in such pleasures. He criticized the conservative minded people in Chile who had their theatres, newspapers and concerts as their pleasures but would deprive the poor people of their reunions, the *Chinganas*. He noted the use of tobacco, smoked in a long stemmed pipe, and the ever-present beverage, beer. He suggests, in his humorous way, that perhaps the origin of the German mystic philosophy can be found in this custom of spending long hours in contemplation of the smoke rings and other fantastic forms it takes. He says he submitted this theory to the professors at the University of Göttingen but that they haven't seen fit to accept it.

Sarmiento was in a hurry to reach Berlin and didn't have time to see the famous museum of Dresden with its rich collection of paintings or the fine books in Leipzig. He traveled by railroad to

Berlin, the most modern of the European capitals. He was impressed with the beautiful city with its wide streets, the trees and the gardens. He found the monuments cold, the new museums and the protestant churches without artistic beauty. However, he was pleased with his reception by the German officials. He had to be careful not to disclose the fact that he was Chilean only by adoption, so high was the praise of the Minister of Instruction for Chile, "considering Chile as an oasis of civilization and order in that desert which begins in Mexico and ends in Buenos Aires." (V, 334)

Sarmiento was assisted in collecting his statistics about education by the Minister of Instruction, Dr. Eikhorn and the chief of statistics, Mr. Dietrice, who helped him in every way. He used the information collected for special studies published in Chile upon his return and later in Argentina. He learned that the Minister of Interior was alarmed at the rate of emigration toward the United States but that it was more desirable than such would be toward South America, which was regarded as the ends of the earth, with bloody revolutions and bad fever infested cities, suffocating heat and poisonous animals. Sarmiento contacted Dr. Wappaus and with him planned studies encouraging emigrants to come to South America.

Sarmiento was very favorably impressed with the results of the German system of education and says:

> Prussia, thanks to its intelligent system of education, is better prepared than France itself for political life, and universal suffrage would not be an exaggeration where all classes have the use of reason, because theirs is cultivated. (V, 335)

After visiting the famous traveler, Baron Humboldt, in Potsdam, Sarmiento arrived at Göttingen, passing by way of Brunswick and Hanover. He spent delightful days in the shadow of this famous, old University. He had been away from Chile now for a long time, he had been in Europe for over a year and he describes the feeling one has in continually traveling from one place to another saying:

> Because finally it becomes sad and distressing to travel about changing places for months and years, with one's heart closed to all affections, floating unknown in a sea of human beings

who go by or remain while you are the one who is passing by, like those strange visions that appear to us in a confused mass during a nightmare! Oh Berlin, Berlin! How I suffered from loneliness there in my heart of hearts! (V, 335)

Göttingen was a small university town, quiet and charming. They received him cordially, and because he was a member of the faculty of the University of Chile, he was invited to an academic act during which a long discourse was given in Latin. Sarmiento says that he hoped he gave a good impression that night because he listened seriously and intently even though he understood not half of the brilliant Latin speech. At any rate he was able to stay awake. He attributes the kindnesses of the professors to their natural curiosity about one from far away America, but that is one of the times when Sarmiento was being modest. He was at home among the academic professors and even though he felt his lack of academic training, he had much to offer to the erudite professors with whom he passed many happy hours. He tells of a deep philosophic discussion the last night before he left when he went out in the garden and looked up at the stars as if searching for the answer to the problems which beset the human mind.

At the end of June or the beginning of July 1847, Sarmiento was back in Paris, visiting Holland and Belgium en route. While he had been traveling in Germany he had received a high honor from the Institute of History in Paris. He was named as a foreign member and this was published in the *Journal de l'Institut Historique* of the 7th of July, 1847.

Back in Paris Sarmiento counted his money. He had only enough left to return home by way of Cape Horn but he already knew this route and would like to see the Isthmus of Panama and the Caribbean and perhaps Mexico. And he didn't want to return without knowing England, which was just across the Channel. And he reasoned, how could one make an inspection trip of education without seeing the United States. Finally, he reached the important decision to go as far as his money lasted and then devote himself to teaching or writing to earn enough to get back to Chile.

Sarmiento tells of his dilemma in Paris as he counted his dwindling dollars. He says that his bankrupt condition only served to whet his appetite and make a good defense of his ideas of seeing England and North America. He felt that he was justified in visiting these places and points out that as a schoolteacher on the lookout for the best in primary education, he could not return to South America without having seen Massachusetts, which had the most progressive schools in the world. Furthermore, there was the subject of immigration. He believed that was the solution to populate the wide expanses of his country. How could he then fail to visit the United States which had an immigration of over two hundred thousand per year? And then, there was the desire to know the republican form of government as practiced in the United States. Having read in Herodotus of those Phoenecians who sailed around Africa, stopping now and then to plant wheat and harvest it in order to continue their voyage, Sarmiento took courage. He came to an important decision and says: "I shall proceed with my watch in one hand and my purse in the other, and should my torch be extinguished . . . I would be left in the dark, and feeling my way with my hands, I would seek my way back to Chile." (V, 441) This was Sarmiento's way of solving the problem. He shows again his faith in himself to forge ahead. He admirably demonstrates his faith in Providence, which his beloved mother, Paula, had instilled in him when a boy, and which time and again had saved him from disaster.

He set out for England, visiting London, Birmingham and Manchester, which itinerary is documented in his diary, now preserved in the Sarmiento Museum. This remarkable record shows the extraordinary frugality of Sarmiento and his careful system of noting all his expenses, even the smallest, in whatever was the currency of the country he was visiting.

In Liverpool Providence began to work. There he ran into an Argentine who was employed in a business firm, Norberto de la Riestra, who took him to his home and helped him secure passage on a large sail boat, the *Montezuma*. There Sarmiento had first hand opportunity to see the emigrants who went to the new world to seek their fortune. He was not dismayed by the poorness of the four hundred and eighty Irish whom he describes:

> In the evenings I would approach the deck, to which the unhappy, naked, haggard Irish, their lives animated by the hope of seeing the end of their wretchedness in the promised land, would come out like rats from their holes. (V, 442)

Rather, he felt happy to think that such a sad specimen of the human race could be assimilated into the growing democracy of the United States. And again, he wondered why the same thing could not happen in the South American countries.

Sarmiento had studied English in 1832 when he was working as a clerk in Valparaiso but he had had little opportunity to perfect his speaking knowledge of it. He had therefore spent most of his time with a Jewish family who spoke French until one day when he was trying to open a door and a fellow passenger spoke to him in Spanish. It was another act of Providence for this man, an Englishman, a Mr. Ward, who was from a business of Huth Gruning in Valparaiso, was able to give Sarmiento the help he needed to visit the United States. Mr. Ward introduced the traveler to a senator from the United States, who was returning from a trip to Europe and he, in turn, gave him a letter of introduction to the one he most wanted to know, Horace Mann, the well-known member of the Board of Education of Massachusetts. Sarmiento landed in New York the last of August, 1847, happy with the prospects of visiting the land he had spent his money to see, instead of returning direct to Chile as one of lesser courage might have done. He says: "My path was gradually becoming clear and every fear, save that of enfeebling my purse, was disappearing by degrees." (V, 442)

PART TWO
Chapter I
FIRST VISIT TO THE UNITED STATES

1. Conditions in the United States

Sarmiento remained in the United States less than three months. It is almost incredible that he was able to see and learn so much in such a short time when there were no airplanes, and trains were much slower than today. He visited all of the large cities and twenty-one of the states. His impressions of his visit fall into two parts, the first part of which is a letter to his friend Don Valentín Alsina, found in *Viajes* pp. 344 - 440, and the second part, consisting of personal anecdotes, *Viajes* pp. 440 - 514. Although more than a hundred years have passed since Sarmiento first visited the United States, this important work still maintains its interest. It is especially notable since it was the first published work about the United States by an Argentine writer. The descriptions are colorful, the judgments are sharp and the writer describes his impressions with an unusual brilliance. Most of all, he was able to interpret clearly the historical phenomenon which was taking place in the new country. Coming from his travels in Europe, he saw clearly the contrasts between the new world and the old. Sarmiento sought the best wherever he went and eagerly tried to transplant it to his country that Argentina might attain the future he dreamed of. After visiting Europe and Africa, he seemed without hope because of the conditions that he had seen, but now he could shout, Eureka! for he had found what he was seeking. Not that he was perfectly satisfied with what he saw, but at least, he saw the germination of what he believed would become the greatest country in the world. For the first time, we find that he wanted to become a part of this great enterprise, for he says that he was overcome with a strange sensation that he had not experienced before, not even in Paris, and it was the secret desire to live forever in the United States, "to become a Yankee." (V, 455) One cannot help wondering what would have been the destiny of Sarmiento had he remained in the country he so admired. However, it was not to be, for his destiny was to be in fighting for those ideas he had seen proved in the United States. It was for him to return to South America with the vision of what education could do for that continent. His work was to be the constant attempt to better the life of his people through education.

New York

Sarmiento arrived at New York at the end of August, 1847. He describes the beauty of the landscape, which reminded him of Rio de Janeiro, even though the colors were less intense and the scenery less grandiose. He remembered the characters of Washington and Franklin as he admired the landscape and remembered their greatness in good natured simplicity, their strength of character, their good sense, their industriousness, and their integrity. He noted the many ships and cites the fact that New York as the port of arrival of European immigrants is the least American of any city in its appearance and customs. He saw the sections of the city with narrow, dirty streets and shabby houses. He saw pigs everywhere and said that no one disputes with them their right to citizenship. But on the other hand, he saw the most beautiful part of the city, Broadway, a wide street which began at Castle Garden and ran north. He was impressed with Trinity Church, a magnificent Gothic structure, built by subscription, an American custom. In one hour on Broadway, he counted four hundred and eighty vehicles which passed his boarding house. One night he went with some new friends, all South Americans, to the theatre in Castle Garden to see *Hernani*. With him were Osma of Peru, Alvear of the Argentine Confederation, Carvallo and his secretary, Astaburuaga, of the Chilean Legation and a world traveler, Santiago Arcos from Chile, who had been trailing Sarmiento since Paris. It must have been a gay night for these young men who greeted the prima donna in Spanish and were rewarded by her ending the performance with Spanish songs and dances. Osma had known her in Spain and also in London. This was the first of the pleasant experiences that Sarmiento was to share with Santiago Arcos, who was to become his traveling companion and a very good friend. Sarmiento went sightseeing with Carvallo, and it was due to his kindness that Sarmiento did not suffer from loneliness as he had during part of his travels in northern Europe. Carvallo invited him to his home and with him visited many schools, factories, monuments and all the points of interest that a traveler should see in and around New York.

Sarmiento describes New York's city building as comparable to the magnificence of that of the Roman Senate, but more than anything he was impressed with the monumental construction of the Croton Dam, which furnished water to New York from five miles up the river. Such feats of engineering he had not seen in Europe and they were not even dreamed of in South America. He learned the measurements and capacity in detail and even the cost of the work, which was thirteen million dollars, the interest of which, along with the salaries of the employees was paid by the municipal tax levied for the use of the water, resulting furthermore in a saving of a half million a year to apply on the principal and furnishing the people with better water than before. While in New York, Sarmiento also visited the cemetery of Brooklyn, Greenwood, which he describes with feeling. Perhaps he was remembering his childhood fear of the cemetery, which his uncle had helped him overcome. Or perhaps it was just his natural curiosity to see one of the differences in the culture of the country.

North of New York and Canada

Sarmiento left his friends to go alone on his pilgrimage to Boston. He had a reason for his strange itinerary, which took him up the Hudson, west to Niagara and then to Canada before he turned back east to arrive finally at Boston. He says that even when study is the object of visiting a place, it is permissible to make side trips in search of picturesque spots. His dwindling purse would not permit many such trips, so that he had to plan to see all that he could for the least possible use of his time and money. He carefully records that he left New York at seven o'clock in the morning for Albany, a hundred and forty-five miles for one dollar, and that he arrived that afternoon in time to take the train for Buffalo, which cost twelve dollars and took him three hundred and twenty-five miles. He describes the Hudson as the center of life of the United States, poetically, historically and commercially.

It is the road to Boston, Montreal, Quebec, to Buffalo, Niagara and the Great Lakes and the principal artery for the products of Canada, Vermont, Massachusetts, New Jersey and New York. He says that its waters were continually covered with ships and that the traffic could be compared to that of the streets of the large cities. Sarmiento was especially impressed with the floating palaces for the transport of passengers. He noted the well-dressed passengers and the general air of politeness and culture, although he says that there is a certain coldness about the Yankee character that indicates a kind of aloofness, although as a matter of fact it is merely a desirable reserve. He noted the landscape along the river and saw the picturesque Palisades, a perpendicular wall of rocks bordering the river for a distance of some twenty miles. He saw the ruins of forts and recalled the names of Washington and Hamilton, and also the military academy of West Point. He says that the Hudson rivaled the Rhine in its beauty, and that only in China could you find the equal of its water traffic.

Sarmiento noted the importance of the location of Buffalo, lying on the eastern shore of Lake Erie and also being the gateway to the west by way of Lakes Huron, Michigan and Superior, and finally to the Mississippi. In addition Buffalo was connected to the Ohio by the Cleveland Canal and to the Hudson by the Erie Canal. In Buffalo, Sarmiento observed that the city was small for its population and he saw the men busily engaged in construction to care for the needs of the city which was growing at the rate of twenty thousand persons every year. He knew that Buffalo was the future center of industry not only because of its location but because of the fact that there was a rich coal supply nearby in the peninsula formed by Lake Michigan and Lake Huron. From Buffalo on, Sarmiento says that the human enterprise, the rail-roads, the new villages and towns detract from the beauty of nature but that north of Buffalo is the most beautiful place on earth.

From Buffalo on, human works, railroads, growing towns and newly planted fields make the sublime works of nature look dull. From there to the north begins the most beautiful piece of land. The Niagara River flows from the mild, crystalline Erie, reflecting in its waves rhododendrons intermixed with oaks, forming distant bluish horizons of primitive forests under whose dense foliage one still can see the mythical tracks of the indomitable Indian's moccasin. It divides, forming the big island and then again gathers its waters to prepare itself for the sublime play of waters that begins at the Rapids and ends with the Cascade. The distant roar of this amazing waterfall, the mist that rises to the sky in aquatic particles, the excitement caused by the nearness of long hoped-for and foreseen sensations make the restless traveler feel that the train is pulling him along too slowly. Finally one reaches Niagara Falls, a town full of spectators, from where the fearful din of the falls thunders in one's ears, the whirlpool of waters becomes more visible, towering in a white mist over the tops of the trees. As you approach, you can see between the tree trunks, contrasting with the opaqueness of their leafy shade, a section of the rapids shining as a piece of burnished silver. These rapids are underwater cascades to which the enormous mass of the Niagara rushes down over steep rocks, which do not appear to the eyes, and give a marble-like whiteness to the water. (V, 449)

Sarmiento had seen other falls but he confesses that this sight made him smile with pleasure but weak at the knees. He describes the awe-inspiring sight of the Falls but says that to really see and feel the Falls, one must put on the rubber cape and boots and descend to the cave at their base. Here is our Sarmiento enjoying his delight in experiencing fear, as in his adventure at Vesuvius.

But you can't hear nor imagine the falls except by going down into the chasm that serves as its base, wrapped up for this purpose in rubber cloaks, led by a guide beneath the very waterfall, where a path has been made in the rock with iron handrails that protect one from falls caused by the presence of hundreds of slippery, slimy eels which take shelter in the curves of the rock. Located in the depths of this unusual gallery, dazed and bewildered by the noise, being lashed all over by heavy jets of water, you see before you a crystal wall that you might think is hard and firm if the filtrations of dripping water did not acknowledge the presence of the liquid element. Having left that damp inferno, seen the sun and sky again, it can be said that your heart has sensed the feeling of something sublime. A battle with two hundred thousand fighters could not cause deeper emotions. (V, 452)

As Sarmiento was traveling in the railroad coach, he remarked from time to time the magnificence of the beauty that he had experienced, when his Yankee listener gave him a new perspective about the Falls.

"Beautiful! Beautiful!" he was saying, and to explain to me his way of sensing beauty, he added: "This cascade is worth millions. Already some machines have been placed along the rapids, from which through inexpensive canals, falls are produced to put them in motion. When the people of the States crowd on this side the huge volume of water from the American cascade can be subdivided, and by deflecting it through canals that will run over the higher land, bring them into the lower river bed of the Niagara to the points where machines for textiles and other industries will be established." He said to me, "Can you imagine that forty thousand horse-power water-driven machines can be used if needed? Then the Niagara will be a street flanked on both sides by seven miles of factories, each with its own waterfall the size the motor needs. Ships will come to anchor at the port and carry merchandise to Europe or New York along the St. Lawrence, Lake Champlain or the Oswego Canal!" (V, 454)

Sarmiento imagined what that region would be when the Yankee prophecy became reality. It was autumn and the trees were in all their glory, just as Cooper had described so vividly in his *Last of the Mohicans*. Sarmiento repeats that this is the most beautiful part of the earth and it was at this moment that he was overcome with a strange sensation that he had not felt before, a desire to live forever in the United States, to become a Yankee and see if he could build a factory beside the Falls. But he says that only a look at his slim purse is enough to cure him of his day dreams and return him to reality.

Sarmiento went on to Montreal and Quebec. He found Montreal the city most modern in respect to civil construction, but says that beneath this there is the moral aspect and laments that this people has kept and cultivated a hopeless ignorance, which he blames on to the Catholic Church. One Sunday he went to the Cathedral to mass and saw that there were some fifteen or twenty thousand persons present and the mass was given by some seventy two priests and altar boys. Such an impressive sight he had not seen even in Europe. However, he could not help observing the backwardness of the Canadians in their poverty, their ignorance, their lack of industry and he felt that in another century, they will have disappeared, incapable of adapting to the present society and hindered by a blind patriotism, which in itself slowly smothers them.

From Montreal, Sarmiento went to Quebec and there he noted the system for receiving the Irish immigrants. The newcomers were housed in barracks, given food and work daily, until they are assigned land in regions selected for the new settlements. Sarmiento, as always, was on the lookout for ideas which he could put into practice in his own country, and says that he sometimes thought that instead of developing new schemes, we should investigate those which have already been proven, such as this.

Sarmiento carefully notes his traveling expenses. A hundred years later they seem insignificant, but we must keep in mind that he was spending the last of the money alloted to him almost two years before. He says that he spent seven dollars for the round-trip excursion from Montreal to Quebec, a city which is not so beautiful but is more modern. Then he adds that he spent one dollar for the train from Buffalo to Niagara Falls, for twenty-two miles; from Niagara Falls to Lewiston, by railroad and stagecoach, six dollars for thirty one miles; Lake Ontario to Montreal, by steamer, ten dollars; from Montreal to La Prairie, by steamer and railroad, one dollar; from La Prairie via Lake Champlain to Whitehall, one dollar; Canal to Troy, three dollars; railroad to Greenbush, three dollars.

Boston

And now he was to visit the Mecca of his pilgrimage, Boston. He describes the Puritan city with its pleasant landscape, the oak under which the pilgrims first met to draw up their basic laws and he remembered that it was in Boston in the year of 1676 that the famous law of compulsory public education was adopted, which initiated the rehabilitation of mankind. He remembered other historic incidents which took place in Boston, the famous Boston Tea Party, and the first shot of the War of Independence. He was no less thrilled to see the magnificent architecture of the public schools of Boston, for the support of which each person paid one dollar each year. Boston was also the center of the Unitarian

creed, which seeks to embrace the many beliefs into a religious
philosophy. From Boston, furthermore, go the colonists who carry
the institutions, science, arts of government and Yankee spirit to
the far west. Boston was also an important port, having four
steamship lines to Europe. There were railroads connecting Boston
to Maine, New Hampshire, Troy, New York, and New York city,
along with excellent water transportation via Long Island Sound.
Sarmiento praised the hotels of Boston, saying that the Tremont
Hotel was superior to any other in comfort and elegance.

But the object of his visit was to meet the well-known educator, Horace Mann, who lived near Boston in East Newton.
Sarmiento describes him as

> The great reformer of primary education, a traveler like me in
> search throughout Europe of methods and systems, and a
> man of inexhaustible source of goodness and philanthropy,
> who brought together in his acts and writings a rare prudence
> and profound knowledge. (V, 464)

Sarmiento spent two days in long conferences with Horace Mann
and learned of his trials and tribulations of his struggle to better
the educational institutions. His labor had been immense but his
financial reward had been slight. However, he was supplementing
the latter by preparing teachers for his country. There, near his
home, he and his wife were training teachers who had paid tuition
to learn mathematics, chemistry, botany and anatomy to round
out their education. They were poor young women who had
borrowed to complete their training, undertaking to repay it as
soon as they were placed as teachers. Since they received good
salaries, there was little risk for the money lenders. Sarmiento
gives the number of schools and teachers in Massachusetts, saying
that in 1846 there were in the 309 cities and towns of this state,
3475 public schools with 2589 men teachers, 5000 women
teachers and 174,084 school children, a number of teachers
greater than the entire standing army of Chile and one-third that
of the United States. Sarmiento says the Yankees have a right to
be proud.

He points out that the state had an average of 100 inhabitants
per square mile, $400 capital per person, an elementary or
secondary school for every 200 inhabitants, an annual income of
five dollars for every child, all this to develop the mind. On the

material side there was the network of railroads, canals and a long seacoast. On the intellectual side there were the churches, the 45 daily newspapers, magazines and reviews, and for the welfare of all, there were educated public officials, frequent meetings in the public interest, as well as religious, philanthropic and other organizations that gave direction and impulse to all. He praised the work of Mr. Mann as secretary of the Board of Education, who travels a part of each year calling educational meetings, and giving lectures on elementary education, demonstrating the advantages to be gained by its diffusion.

Sarmiento was pleased with his meeting with Horace Mann. He received letters of introduction to many prominent persons and Sarmiento says that the letters alone were all that were necessary for him to be received cordially everywhere. Later Sarmiento was to declare himself a disciple of Horace Mann and also to write his biography but, as we shall see, the fame of the disciple was destined to become greater than that of the master.

While Sarmiento was in Boston, he visited Lowell, an important textile center. Here he was again favorably impressed by what he describes as the high intelligence of the people. He compared the conditions of the American workers with the miserable factory workers of England, and pointed out that the original cost of the transportation from the southern states to England and to Massachusetts varied little and that the difference lay in the salaries paid and that the Lowell textiles were able to compete in price and quality with the English textiles. Sarmiento says that this was due to the intelligence of the workers and to their education, which enabled them to work more efficiently and to produce a better and larger quantity of work.

He was interested in seeing the girls who had left their homes to come to the city to work and save money to set up their homes. He describes their dress and manners, saying that they dress well, wear silk hose and shawls on Sundays and carry a parasol. They live in large hotels where they have economical food and lodging as well as libraries, newspapers and even pianos. He says that they were educated girls and that their modest habits protect them from loose living and that they see in the men about them only candidates for husbands. He says that Lowell is a model of what a city can be when capital combines with the social evolution of labor in industry.

After seeing all the worthwhile sights, Sarmiento left by railroad and boat to return to New York. He says that he was still remembering the most impressive two weeks journey that can be made, and was seeing yet in his imagination Niagara Falls, when he went to see a performance featuring the midget, Thom Thumb.

From Boston to New York and Washington

Sarmiento humorously describes his next meeting with his Chilean friend, Santiago Arcos, who was impatient about starting the homeward journey. As a matter of fact, Sarmiento was almost down to his last dollar and it was Providence working again that had brought him in contact with one who could befriend him in his necessity. He tells of their meeting with the candid manner that so characterizes him, even when discussing such a personal situation as being without money in a foreign land.

Don Santiago Arcos was awaiting me impatiently so that we could undertake the return trip to Chile. Every time he spoke to me of the matter, I would put on the expression of a cabinet minister when he does not know if he will remember or not what is being requested of him. We would open the map, trace the route, and we were almost on our way, without my giving any signs of agreeing to anything. Finally I had to explain. I had twenty-two guineas and about thirty one-peso paper notes in a cash box, not a penny more. Finally I took my decision in hand and exposed my financial situation with all the dignity of one who neither asks nor accepts help, intimating my decision to go my own way on from Havana to continue through Caracas. Arcos had listened to me with interest and even was tempted by the prospect of crossing the tropical solitudes of South America, risking unknown adventures, suffering hardships and not depending on anyone but himself to overcome them, but the romantic and virile side of his character is no less apparent than the joviality and frankness that mark him. When I was expecting offers and protests he came out with a pantomime dance and side-splitting laughter that made me lose my dignity again. "How fine!" he kept saying, jumping and laughing; "why, I have only four hundred pesos! Let us form a company and when the capital we both have is exhausted, we shall provide ourselves according to the seriousness of the situation." (V, 469-470)

They decided that Sarmiento should continue his travels to Washington, by way of Philadelphia and Baltimore, and then meet in Philadelphia to start the homeward journey via Harrisburg and Pittsburgh, down the Ohio and the Mississippi to New Orleans. In the pooling of resources, Sarmiento turned over his bills and the guineas to have changed, and then borrowed from Arcos thirty-four dollars for the expenses of this trip. However, this incident proved to be the origin of difficult moments later on in his journey.

In Baltimore, Sarmiento took the train for Washington but because a bridge had been washed out by heavy rains, the Washington bound train a short time out of Baltimore encountered the previous train returning to Baltimore. Sarmiento describes the panic stricken passengers, waving handkerchiefs as they fearfully expected a head-on collision. Sarmiento tells of the passengers lifting the locomotive and tender and dragging them to the rear of the train in order to return to Baltimore. There he took a steamboat to Washington, to arrive by way of the Chesapeake Bay and the Potomac River. En route, Sarmiento experienced another of the adventures which may befall one traveling in a foreign country, where one does not know the customs or the language. He describes the poor accommodations of the steamboat, and says that the cabins were filled with rows of bunks of six or seven stacked one upon the other, like drawers in a cabinet. The steward gave him his in the fifth row. He passed the day viewing the landscape but when night came, he was ready to go to sleep. He was wondering how to reach his bunk and suddenly resolved to climb up to it. He says he was climbing up, lizard fashion, when he heard below him the sound of voices and laughter. In fact, he had one leg inside his bunk, when someone took him by the other leg and commenced letting him know in no uncertain terms that the bunk was his and that he had placed his handkerchief there as evidence of possession. All of this was totally incomprehensible to Sarmiento, whose English was negligible. But when he looked down below, he saw the crowd laughing at him. He says that there was nothing for him to do but come down, hide his face between his hands, and go jump in the river. But he did not go to that extreme. Instead he went to a place where the light was well directed upon his face and started speaking in French, asking if there were anyone in the group who spoke French or Spanish. A deep silence pervaded the group who moments before had been amused. Presently, he heard his words translated into English. Then the crowd changed completely. They were sorry that he had taken so seriously their amusement which was without malice, for Sarmiento says that the Yankee has a kind heart. The crowd pressed upon him cordially and the one who claimed the disputed bunk tried to explain in a calm manner what had happened. The steward explained to all that he had given the bunk to Sarmiento, and then gave him another one, which turned out to be better than the original one which had been the subject of dispute.

Washington

The following day Sarmiento reached Washington. He refers to his stay there as one of his happiest during his travels in distant lands. He was a guest in the home of the Chilean Minister, Carvallo, where he was received most cordially and had as his guide the secretary of the Chilean Legation, Astaburuaga. Astaburuaga accompanied Sarmiento in his sight-seeing around Washington and pointed out to him the young women who were to be seen in the street, one as Astaburuaga pointed out, the daughter of a Senator, another, the daughter of a banker, another, a seamstress or a young woman of less social position. Sarmiento noted their simple dress, their manner of moving about in the street alone, stopping to look at whatever they wished, and says that this gives an idea of the respect enjoyed by the North American woman as well as the liberty a single woman has.

Astaburuaga wanted Sarmiento to know the editor of the *Washington Intelligencer*, an important opposition newspaper of the capital. Sarmiento spent many hours with Mr. Johnson, a Whig and a son of a General of the same name of the Revolutionary War. He says that they passed many hours in hot discussions and Sarmiento was surprised to find in the United States a detractor of democracy and the republic. Sarmiento says that when he tried to argue with him, he was told that he must not be deluded by the appearance of order, prosperity and progress nor attribute such to the form of government, because beneath the surface there was only misery, meanness, ignorance and selfishness, and that he must not return to South America with the idea of taking the United

States as a model. At other times he was not so radical and confessed that he tended to exaggerate because he felt the tyranny of the party in power and that he as the son of a famous general and having a better education, should occupy a better position. Sarmiento differed with him on many points in political theory and one of those was in the idea of liberty. Sarmiento maintained that history proves to be a kind of moral geology, with improvement and progress evident and that no civilization has reverted to cannibalism, once it progressed beyond it.

> As soon as there is a school in a town, newspapers in a city, a ship on the sea, and a hospital for the sick, democracy and equality will begin to exist. The result of all this is that the mass being formed is immense, for these are no nations or peoples as such and individual freedom is upheld everywhere by the entire civilized humanity; and whenever there should be a public inclined to enter the fatal cycle of despotism assigned to it, the spectacle and influence of one hundred others who enter the period of liberty will hold it back from the fatal precipice. (V, 483-484)

Johnson, on the other hand, believed that liberty led to license, license led to anarchy, and that anarchy in turn led to despotism. Nothing could have pleased Sarmiento more than to be involved in such discussions. He was in his element when he was discussing political problems and none was better equipped than he, both for his study and his recent travel experience, to judge what he saw in practice. Surely we can feel Sarmiento's admiration for what he had seen in the United States notwithstanding Mr. Johnson's contradiction, for he said that in the United States, you do not have war, nor classes, nor aristocracy, nor a populace in the old Roman sense, but a nation, with equal rights for all, individual industriousness, machinery to aid in work, railroads, telegraph, printing presses, schools, colleges, asylums, hospitals, penitentiaries, etc., all of which occupy half a continent. It was Sarmiento's belief that all would arrive to this level of civilization.

Sarmiento describes the buildings in Washington, the wide streets, the parks and the Capitol. He said that at the time of his visit, there was being installed an electric light which was to illuminate the dome and he said that such indeed was a beautiful symbol for that building whose light of intelligence shines to illuminate the entire nation. He thought that the White House was modest and not in keeping with the dignity of the president of the United States. Sarmiento says that the president receives without ceremony anyone who desires to see him and during one day of the week and on several special occasions of the year, anyone can enter the White House.

While in Washington, Sarmiento paid a visit to that shrine which is Mount Vernon,

> Fifteen miles from Washington is Mount Vernon, the home and tomb of that great man whom all the human race has accepted as a saint; great because of his virtue and the greatest of men for having placed the cornerstone of the building of the only nation in the world that clearly sees its future and whose future is the beautiful ideal of greatness of modern nations. (V, 484)

Sarmiento describes the emotion which he felt upon arriving at Mount Vernon, where he said he removed his hat and walked with reverence, as if he were stepping upon sacred land. He describes the home of Washington as being spacious and elegant but with extreme simplicity. But it was the tomb, which moved him saying,

> How much art is not revealed in the location of this tomb, how much grandeur in its darkness, and how American and national is that accompaniment of primeval forests, rustic torrents and little streams in the state of nature! (V, 485)

Sarmiento, who had seen the marvels of art of the old world, discusses the artistic development which he notes in the United States.

> And still Washington, the hero of North American independence, the founder of the positive and hard-working nation, was also destined to inspire the feeling for fine arts in the children of the Puritans. . . . The North Americans believe they have no artistic vocation and pretend to disdain art works as the result of ancient societies corrupted by luxury. I have thought, however, that I came upon the deep, exquisite feeling for beauty and greatness in these people who move ahead rapidly in search of material well-being, and in their

path leave all their works incomplete and half-finished.
Doesn't moral beauty have any place in the feeling for the
ideal of beauty? What people in the world have felt more
deeply this need for comfort, decency, leisure, well-being,
cultivation of the intellect? What people has felt more horror
at the sight of ugliness, poverty, ignorance, drunkenness,
physical and moral degradation which is like the core and
primary appearance of European societies? In Rome, amid
monuments and basilicas, they stretch out their well-kept
hands begging alms. (V, 486-487)

Sarmiento also says that the artistic indications as revealed in
the monumental buildings, wharves, aquaducts and statues erected
in Boston, Philadelphia and New York are expressions of the
American feeling for art but they do not constitute such, which he
calls the constant aspiration on the part of the people for a national conception, embodied in and revealed by every citizen
through successive generations. And for this he says that the
American genius is present in a model of a monument to be
erected to the memory of the great American hero, Washington,
which will be two meters higher than the pyramid of Cheops in
Egypt. And it is in this that he finds the Yankee genius.

Two meters above the tallest monument built by men, I be-
hold the unrivalled grandeur, typical of that nation, a feeling
that has preceded or followed the greatest periods that some
part of the human race have reached. (V, 489)

The idea of erecting the monument to Washington, Sarmiento
says, was received with enthusiasm throughout the country,
because it harmonized with the national aspiration to surpass
other nations. Furthermore, he adds that the financial provision
for the Washington Monument is another side of the Yankee's
artistic genius, for the colossal monument is to be raised by popular subscription of only a few cents from each contributor.

So each year the public in large numbers brings to the feet of
the statue of the great man, a kind of beautiful national ideal,
a spontaneous tribute of gratitude and homage, and on this
point all the nations on earth can surrender. . . . Stones with
inscriptions sent by all the States of the Union, cities, cor-

porations, scientific, philanthropical and even industrial societies should decorate the interior of the Washington Monument. That system of popular and spontaneous contribution for the realization of a national thought contributes, in my opinion, the clearest example of the existence of a national artistic feeling. (V, 490-491)

He tells of the museums, which contain a mixture of works of art and curiosities, and which are springing up throughout the country, the admittance fees to which are used to enrich the collections. He describes the sensation that a beautiful nude statue of the young American artist, Poper, created upon being exhibited in New York. After a few days, he says, the prudes raised their eyes and accustomed themselves to gaze at the artistic beauty in that marble mirror, and when the curiosity was satisfied in New York, the exhibit took to the road where it was gaped at by the rude eyes of the people and earned considerable money as a reward for the talented artist. Sarmiento believes that such customs are more powerful stimuli and ovation to American art than kings have been able to stimulate by spending for the encouragement of the fine arts, not their own money but that wrung from their people for their own selfish pleasures.

Sarmiento predicts that the day will come when the great artists of Europe will take their masterpieces on tour in the United States earning thousands of dollars and educating the American taste, and later seeking the approval that the people will pay to talent. Already, he says, the celebrated singers and dancers are beginning to point the way that painters and sculptors will follow. Even the idea of the traveling art exhibitions has been followed in the development of magnificent floating theatres which give plays at important towns and cities on both banks of a large river. Sarmiento thinks that the North Americans have customs which lead to the development of the arts, saying that the strenuous life they lead and the excitement of business constantly spur them on to travel which fills an emotional need. This sightseeing and traveling takes the people to Niagara Falls, the coastal cities and the Great Lakes, or the older part of the United States which exercises an important moral influence upon the inland population, because it is the centre of intellectual and commercial interests as well as the capital of the government.

Sarmiento would like to see Washington become a center of

art and he had many worthwhile suggestions to offer.

> Washington, the nominal capital of the Union, will no doubt profit in the near future from these dispositions of the national spirit if the Capitol, Museum of Inventions and the monument erected to Washington, are accompanied by other attractions that will finally make the capital a center of pageantry that arouses the curiosity of travelers and awakens nationalism. Home of the senators, cabinet members and high officials as well as of representatives of other nations, Washington could enhance its evening entertainment with opera, dramatic arts and ballets, if religious ideas did not oppose them so strongly. The North Americans as a nation ought to undertake the conquest of the monuments of European arts. . . . One hundred thousand dollars annually, destined for the acquisition of the works of old and modern masters, would provide the basis of the future American art in the United States. Washington ought to show the perfect limitations, as if it were a school, of the Rotunda of Agrippa, the Parthenon of Athens, the Cathedral of Rouen as a model of Gothic, and of half a dozen more celebrated buildings. Thus that little town which is not good for anything now, being contrary to time and progress, would at a glance enlarge and beautify all American cities, and would become an artistic capital. (V, 493-495)

Sarmiento visited the Patent Office in Washington and found there the progress that he so admired. He says that the North Americans have done as they should do in everything related to culture:

> In this field of intellectual activity of the country they proceeded, as they ought to, in everything related to culture, namely: first importing, plagiarizing, plundering the other nations to enrich their spirit with data and act later. (V, 495)

He said that in the Patent Office you could trace the history of the progress which the industrial arts have undergone since its establishment, and he gives the number of patents issued for inventions and improvements up to the year 1844 as 13,523, of which 531 were issued in the year 1843. Sarmiento quotes from proceedings of the House of Commons in England concerning exportation of machinery in which it was admitted that the majority of new machinery consisted of inventions which came principally from America. Sarmiento says that it is admitted that

Today North America invades the world, more with products and inventions, and with engineers, craftsmen and machinists who set out to teach the arts of producing much at low cost, attempting everything and attaining wonders. (V, 495-496)

Sarmiento says that not only in the field of useful arts but also in the intellectual field, Americans are beginning to make a place for themselves. He says that the number of books published during the twelve years prior to 1842 consisted of 106 original books on biography, 118 on American geography and history, 91 on the geography and history of other lands, 19 on philosophy, 123 on poetry, and 115 novels. Almost at the same time there were reprinted in England 382 original books from the United States, when twenty years before a reviewer had asked, "Who reads American books?" Sarmiento says that the orators and statesmen who equal Everett, Webster, Calhoun, and Clay are possessed only by England and France and that public speaking, as in France, is beginning to be a stepping stone to power and influence. The American travelers, naturalists, archaeologists, geologists and astronomers who are undertaking to enrich science are showing by the results obtained that they are much more advanced than Europe would like to believe.

Sarmiento says that perhaps one will ask why he has discussed the intellectual progress of the country along with his description of his trip to Washington, but that he has done so in order to give a kind of a unity to such reminiscences even though they have nothing in common with the capital.

From Washington to Cincinnati

Sarmiento stayed in Washington a day longer than he had planned and thus began another of the adventures which characterize his travels. He had arranged with his Chilean friend, Arcos, to meet in Harrisburg at the United States Hotel. But when he arrived there, he learned that there was no United States Hotel. Sarmiento says that he had selected that name as the meeting place since he had seen hotels by that name everyplace, he supposed that there would be one in Harrisburg. Finally, after much difficulty, he found a message from Arcos in the Post House Hotel telling him that he would await him in Chambersburg. Considerably upset by this unexpected turn of events, Sarmiento proceeded to Chambersburg but was unable to find him there. Sarmiento says that Arcos spoke English so well that nobody would have recognized him as a Spaniard and that his (Sarmiento's) English must have shaken the poor Yankees to the very core. He thought that perhaps Arcos had gone on a hunting trip, because they had planned one, but he was not to be found. Finally, Sarmiento learned that he had left a message at the post office and that message said that he would await him in Pittsburgh, which was 150 miles away. Then Sarmiento was really distressed because to cross the Alleghenies to arrive at Pittsburgh, he would have to take the stagecoach and he had no money to pay his passage. In fact, he had only three or four dollars, hardly enough to pay his hotel bill. He learned that Arcos had left on the stagecoach, riding on the top on a bag of hay, when he had not been able to secure a seat, all because he couldn't wait eight hours, the time when the next train would leave. It was another of the mishaps which might befall any traveler and those who have traveled and run out of money, will understand the predicament that Sarmiento was in.

> Here I am, then, in the heart of the United States, inland, so to speak, without a cent, making myself understood with much difficulty and surrounded by those indifferent, icy American faces. What fear and anxieties I experienced in Chambersburg! I was constantly calling the owner of the hotel and by word or writing would explain my situation to him. A young man ahead of me takes my money, unaware that I do not have the amount needed for travel expenses. At the Post House they ask me for ten dollars for the passage and I have only four dollars to pay for the hotel. But I have a few objects of intrinsic value in my suitcase and I want the Post House to keep them until I have covered my passage to Pittsburgh. On hearing this sad story, all the innkeeper would do was to shrug his shoulders in reply. I told my troubles to the coach driver and he would stand there looking at me as if I had said nothing to him. (V, 497-498)

Finally they suggested to Sarmiento that he send a telegram to his friend. This he did and not withstanding the necessity for brevity, he commenced his telegram with: "Don't be a swine," and told of his misfortune. He didn't know whether or not there was a United States Hotel in Pittsburgh, so he suggested that Arcos be looked for in the principal hotels of that city. The reply was delayed and Sarmiento was wondering if he would ever catch up with his friend. Finally, the reply came but it was useless. Arcos had not been found but they had sent to look for him again. Two hours later another message came — "There is no such person!" Sarmiento says that he stood as though struck by lightning. Then someone mentioned Philadelphia and he asked, "Why Philadelphia?" So it happened that they had sent the telegram to Philadelphia, because the stagecoach passage is paid for in Philadelphia. They were going to telegraph Pittsburgh but as they got to the door, they stopped short. The office was already closed until the following morning at eight o'clock. We can well imagine Sarmiento's rage.

> The grand passions of the soul cannot be unburdened except in the native language, and though English has a possible *God damn* for special cases, I preferred Spanish which is so rotund and sonorous for letting out a howl of fury. The Yankees are not much accustomed to the show of Latin passions, and the host, hearing me curse in deep excitement in a foreign language, looked at me in amazement, and making a sign with his hand as if to stop me a moment before I would bite everyone or commit suicide, rushed out into the street in search of a policeman no doubt to arrest me. That's all I needed! And that idea suddenly brought back my composure which I had lost for a moment in my anxiety. (V, 499)

A few minutes later, the innkeeper returned, accompanied by a man with a pen stuck behind his ear. Sarmiento says that this person coldly asked him, first in English, then in French and then in halting Spanish what the difficulty was. Sarmiento says that he explained in a few words what had happened and begged him to intercede with the postal authorities to accept his watch and other valuables as a pledge until he had repaid his fare in Pittsburgh.

That fellow listened to me without moving a muscle of his

impassible face, and when I had finished talking said to me in
French: "Sir, the only thing I can do . . . (What an introduction! I said to myself, swallowing saliva.) . . . the only thing I
can do is pay for the hotel and your passage to Pittsburgh,
provided that when you have arrived in that city you deposit
in the Merchants-Manufactory Bank to the account of Lesley
and Co. of Chambersburg the amount you think necessary to
pay you here in advance." — I had to take a deep breath to
answer him: "But, sir, thanks, but you do not know me and
if I can give you some guarantee" . . . "It is not worth the
trouble; people in your situation, sir, never deceive." (V,
499-500)

The man left and the first thing Sarmiento did was to eat
twenty-five cents' worth of apples, for the series of events of the
past three days had awakened his hunger. He walked around the
city and enjoyed the sensation of again being his own master. In
the early evening his guardian angel reappeared, laden with books,
some in Italian and some in French. He spoke with him both in
Spanish and French and told Sarmiento that he knew Latin and
Greek. He made a few inquiries about Sarmiento's travels and
retired, wishing him a good night. The next morning, he came
again and gave Sarmiento four five dollar bills, one of which
Sarmiento wanted to return as unnecessary. But as he was about
to leave, he insisted on giving Sarmiento another five dollar bill.
Sarmiento understood the delicate feeling that had prompted his
offer, and after resisting feebly, accepted it cordially.

The stagecoach departed at last and he regained his usual peace
of mind, congratulating himself on having had the opportunity,
although one quite painful to him, to bring out the sympathy so
noble of Mr. Lesley. He tells of the night in another of his
descriptions that are almost poetry. As they reached the summit, a
woman's voice spoke to him in French and asked him to get out to
see the view.

I took advantage of the advice, got off after the others, and
actually enjoyed one of the most beautiful and peaceful
spectacles of nature. The Allegheny Mountains are covered to
the top with a thick, leafy vegetation; the tops of the trees on
the foothills, lighted from above by the moon, presented the
appearance of a shadowy blue sea which, because of the

continual change of the spectator, was gradually increasing its silent dark waves, causing that excitement which the sight of such well-known and understood objects arouses in the soul while they cannot be well discerned, because either the eye cannot see so far or the light is faint and wavering. (V, 501)

Later on during the journey, the same lady spoke to him again and asked him if he had been in some difficulty. He answered her negatively and the conversation ended there, but she asked to be excused if it were an indiscreet question, stating that she could not help hearing his conversation with another gentleman, since she had happened to be in the next room. He told her that everything had been taken care of. But she continued, asking him what he would do if he failed to find his friend in Pittsburgh. He told her that her question terrified him and that he had not even given such a possibility a thought, but that he would have to return to Washington or New York, where he had friends.

And why would he not continue his journey? — Why must I engulf myself, madam, in a strange land without any funds? — I was telling you this because my house is five leagues this side of New Orleans and I wanted to offer you hospitality. From there you can get news of your friend and if you should not find him, write to your country and wait for them to send you what you need. — The noble act of Mr. Lesley had obviously been contagious. That lady had heard everything and wanted to repeat the good deed. (V, 501-502)

Sarmiento was touched by her kindness. She quickly explained that her husband had passed away only six weeks before and she was en route to New Orleans to put his affairs in order. Her nine-year-old daughter was traveling with her and both were dressed in deep mourning. Sarmiento says that it was the mother and not the woman who had offered her home to a stranger, who must have had also a mother, and that idea sanctified her offer, but that he was certain that the possibility she had imagined would not arise.

In Pittsburgh, Sarmiento went to find Arcos. Fortunately, there was a United States Hotel in Pittsburgh and Sarmiento found him in the act of writing an advertisement to inform Sarmiento of his whereabouts. He had arrived in a frame of mind to scold him for his childish act, which had caused him so much trouble, but that when saw the comically anguished expression on Arcos' face, he could not help laughing and extending his hand. They set out immediately to tell the lady who had taken passage on the steamship *Martha Washington* so that she need not depart worrying. Sarmiento tells that when she greeted him she tried to slip a bag of gold to him without being seen but that he didn't accept it. He introduced Arcos and both he and Arcos expressed a thousand thanks for her kindness. He has even forgotten her name and it would appear that ingratitude is the compensation for her disinterested kindness. They separated in Cincinnati, never to meet again.

From Cincinnati to New Orleans

Sarmiento and Arcos spent four or five days in Cincinnati where they wandered through the streets, visited the museums and enjoyed the sights. Sarmiento was impressed by the growth of Cincinnati, which was a village in 1789 and became a city in 1819. He noted that there were means of communication with every port, canals, railroads and macadamized and dirt roads. From its port, steamboats left every day for Pittsburgh, and others went downstream to St. Louis and New Orleans. He felt that the most distinctive feature of Cincinnati was its large number of literary, scientific, and philanthropic societies. He cites a law concerning the payment of taxes on unimproved land, and says that such a law prevents wealthy landowners from monopolizing land solely to profit by rising value given to it by the mere passage of time, because if they are delinquent in payment of taxes, the sheriff seizes a portion of their land and sells it. He describes Cincinnati as the center of the hog industry, where there is a group of the local society called the "pork aristocracy." He says that ownerless pigs by the thousands live in the streets and the citizens may select one to fatten at home, the children ride on them when they can catch them, and when they propagate too freely, the police order them to be destroyed.

It was also in Cincinnati that Arcos, seeing a peaceful Yankee sitting reading his Bible in front of his shop, took the cigar that he was smoking out of his mouth to light his own, put the cigar back into the good man's mouth, and went on his way without the Yankee's raising his eyes or making any other movement than to open his mouth for the cigar. Sarmiento noted that incident saying that he received patience in return for his impertinence.

They boarded the steamship for New Orleans, the third to go down the river since news had been received that yellow fever epidemic which ravages that city every summer had ceased. The distance from Cincinnati to New Orleans was 1548 miles and the trip was made in 11 days, traveling day and night and making stops only to pick up passengers or load wood. The trip including the passage, board and service cost $15, or less than the cost to live in a hotel for the same length of time. Sarmiento says that he can tell little about the cities at whose ports and wharves the steamboat stopped, for they stayed at none long enough for him to retain a distinct recollection of them. They passed Marietta, Louisville, Rome and Cairo and then the scene took on a wild, semi-savage character as the frontier of the far west began.

The voyage on the Mississippi is one of the most beautiful and has left me the most enduring and peaceful memories. The majestic river descends gently and rippling through the heart of the largest valley on earth. The scenery changes with each wave and the moderate width of the largest of rivers allows the eye to see on this bank or the other the dark vine-covered forests and to scan the flat lands and openings that the main vegetation makes from time to time. Meeting a ship is a desired incident because of the nearness and rapidity of the passage, while the eyes look down from the top of the galleries of the floating palace on a squadron of barges loaded with coal coming downstream with the current. Farther on you see a small boat or a merchant who goes along in his little sailboat telling jokes and selling trinkets in the neighboring villages. To go ashore at cities and towns where the steamer would stop, to run through the streets, to go into a mine, to pry into everything, to buy apples and cookies, with an ear attentive to the bell that announces departure, was a pleasant variation that never stopped adding to our emotions, just as we never failed to jump over a ravine, to reach the forest and run a while, as long as the steamer was loading firewood to burn in its giant boilers. (V, 509)

As Sarmiento approached New Orleans, he noted the plantations with the rows of wooden cottages on them, all of the same

shape and size, showing that free choice did not guide their construction, and the larger houses, the mansions of the landowners.
This was the cotton and the sugar aristocracy, but with the
product of the slaves' labor. Sarmiento felt that this was the deep,
incurable sore that threatened gangrene to the robust body of the
Union. He says what a fatal mistake it was of Washington and the
other great leaders who made the declaration of the rights of man
to let the southern planters keep their slaves. He felt that it was
the more serious because in the United States there has been made
the greatest progress in the ideals of equality and charity, and says
that the United States are destined to have the last battles against
the ancient injustice of man to man, already conquered in the rest
of the earth. He felt that a racial war of extermination would
come within a century, or else a mean, black backward nation
would be found alongside a white one — the most powerful and
cultivated on earth. He felt that slavery was a parasite growth
which the English colonization left on the luxuriant trees of
American liberties, and which was not cut out at the roots because
they were waiting for it to die by itself, but which instead now
threatens to kill the tree. Sarmiento felt that this problem was one
of the gravest ones, which cast a dark shadow over an otherwise
brilliant and radiant future of the United States.

Sarmiento describes the city of New Orleans, its magnificent
port and the hundreds of boats, and says that the steamboat was
invented for the Mississippi. He envisions the time when the river
will be covered by thousands of steamboats, providing the only
water outlet to the sea for a world to be, when the great
Mississippi valley is populated.

Sarmiento and Arcos stayed in New Orleans for ten days until
they secured passage to Havana. Sarmiento says that it was a
terrible sailboat and like the one which had carried him from
Mallorca to Argel, it had its cargo of hogs, along with some dying
consumptives who shared the narrow cabins, which were very hot
and full of spider webs. Sarmiento says that he felt the North
American world ending and began to feel the presence of the
Spanish colonies, to which they were going.

2. Impressions

In his letter to Valentín Alsina, written on the 12th of
November 1847, Sarmiento gives his impressions about what he

has just seen in the United States. This letter is found in *Viajes* pp. 344 - 440 and much of it has been very ably translated in *A Sarmiento Anthology* pp. 193 - 228. Here Sarmiento comments upon everything that he saw. The length of the letter gives an indication of how much he had seen and written about. He was favorably impressed with almost all that he saw but he didn't hesitate to say what he did not like.

He left the United States sad, thoughtful, pleased, and humbled, with half of his illusions gone and the rest confused. This country seemed to him to have no precedent, to be a kind of an extravaganza that shocks at first sight because it runs counter to all preconceived ideas. He says that in order to learn how to observe it, one must first educate one's own judgment to overlook its apparent organic defects in order to appreciate its true character. But he warns that the risk must be run in becoming deeply attached to it, following the first surprise, and proclaims a new judgment about human affairs just as the romantic movement did in order to have its own monstrosities pardoned when it overthrew the old idol of Franco-Roman poetry. Sarmiento says that the Republic exists even though it is not perfect and that in the United States there is democracy so that the Republic dreamed of will come later. From whatever point of view, the United States seem to him a great nation. The Americans show in their undertakings, plans and work a virility which leaves the rest of the human race far behind, Sarmiento says. And considering that this is a new country, with iron and coal, popular education, religious liberty and political liberty, he was confident that the day was not far off when there would exist a strong republic, the choice of hundreds of millions. He says that this is certain because the progress of the North American people is proven; the population increases a hundredfold, meanwhile the other nations increase as one; but even these numeric factors don't express in themselves the productive force, the moral and physical energy of a nation accustomed to practices of liberty, work and union.

Geographical Blessings

Sarmiento says that if God were to entrust him with the formation of a great republic, he would not undertake such a difficult task unless he were granted certain physical conditions:

If God should entrust me to form a great republic, our very own republic, for example, I would not accept such a charge except on condition that He give me these basic facts at least: unlimited space so that one day two hundred million inhabitants could enjoy it; ample exposure to the seas and coasts indented with gulfs and bays; a varied surface not offering difficulties to railroads and canals that will cross the state in all directions; and since I shall never consent to suppressing railroad affairs, there must be enough coal and iron so that in the year 4751 the mines will still be working as on the first day. The great abundance of lumber would be the only obstacle I would allow for the easy clearing of the land, personally taking charge of giving opportune direction to navigable rivers that would cross the country in all directions, to become lakes where the outlook required it, all flowing into the seas, bringing together all climates so that the products of the poles should come straight to the tropical countries and vice versa. Then for my future designs I would request abundance of marble, granite, porphyry and other stones without which nations cannot imprint upon the forgetful land their eternal mark. (V, 346-347)

Sarmiento says that if one would doubt such possibility, he is foolish because it is the United States just as God created it.

The United States is, just as God has formed it, and to declare that when creating this piece of the world He knew very well that around the 19th century the outcasts of poor humanity, downtrodden in other places, enslaved or starving so that the few could have leisure, would come together here, developing without restraint, grow great and by their example avenge the human species for many centuries of unfair bondage and sufferings. Why did the Romans not discover that land so eminently adaptable to industry which they did not practice, to the peaceful invasion of the colonist and so bountiful to the individual? Why did the Anglo-Saxon race stumble upon this corner of the world which was so well suited to the industrial instincts; and why did the Spanish race have the good fortune of South America where there were silver and gold mines, mild and servile Indians who were precious assets compared with the laziness of their masters, their backwardness, their industrial ineptitude? Is there perhaps no order or premeditation in all this? Is there no Providence? Oh, my friend, God is the easiest solution to all these difficulties! (V, 347)

Communication System

Sarmiento says that the Yankees would have been very stupid if they had failed to complete the plan of Providence by building canals, so that merchandise from Canada could arrive at New York or New Orleans, traveling by inland navigation. Moreover, he adds that since the American state must live by exporting its raw materials, its principal need is for a network of communications. He predicts the day when with the increase of wealth and population, the coastal cities will no longer be the only centers of wealth. He thought that one of the most likely centers, because it has transportation facilities and an abundance of raw materials, would be Pittsburgh. He describes the wealth of the coal supply which is there, saying that area is some 14,000 square miles, or almost the size of England. Because of its location, it can receive cotton which comes up the river and with the superior machinery, it can produce in its many factories much woven and printed cotton goods. He points out that Pittsburgh at the end of the last century was still in the hands of the Indians, and that in 1845 the population had grown to about 45,000.

In discussing the movement of population westward, which Sarmiento describes as advancing toward the Pacific at the rate of five hundred miles each year, he says that a new industrial center farther west will be essential later on. And to that necessity, Providence already has arranged another coal deposit of some sixty thousand square miles near the convergence of the Missouri and Ohio rivers with the Mississippi.

Sarmiento saw the Great Lakes region as the center of a gigantic union and noted the advantages of the natural resources of that region. He says that the railroad brings to Buffalo and the Great Lakes region each day hundreds of people who have come from Europe to choose some piece of forest land on which to settle a new family.

A similar confusion of tongues among those who come, although the land imposes its own language after a short time, and like water rubbing against the sharp surfaces of many stones forming pebbles, as if they were one family, thus joining one another, mixing with each other, these groups of parts of old societies form the new one, the youngest and most daring republic in the world. (V, 351)

Sarmiento asks if it is not singular that the United States should have the glory of inventing both the lightning rod and ethers, which have spared humanity two great scourges and have given planetary speed to man's movements by the application of steam to river vessels invented by Fulton and of electric telegraphy by Morse. He describes the use made of the telegraph system in France, where it was limited to service for the government and compares it with the circuits of wires which cover the United States and link the cities together.

Sarmiento says that Nature brought the great territory of the Union into being, but that without the profound economic science possessed by the Americans the work would have remained incomplete. He states that besides the network of telegraph wires that cover the country, there are 142,295 miles of roads over which the mail coaches carry correspondence daily, canals totaling 853 miles, and railroads too numerous to enumerate, which give each state, city and village easy access to speedy, daily transportation cheap enough for everyone.

Villages

Sarmiento was impressed by the villages and says that the American villages, contrary to those of other nations, are the centers of political life, just as the family is the center of domestic life. He said that the United States can be found in complete miniature in its villages.

The North American village is an entire state, with its civil government, newspaper, schools, banks, municipal government, census, spirit and appearance. From the heart of the primitive forest, stagecoach or wagons set out for a small clearing in the center of which stand ten or twelve houses. These are brick, built with the help of machines which give the sides the smoothness of mathematical figures, held together by very fine straight lines of mortar. They are two stories high covered with painted wooden roofs. Doors and windows painted white, closed and locked with visible locks, and green stores give life and variety to the regularity of the distribution. I note these details because they alone suffice to characterize a people and arouse a number of thoughts. (V, 353-354)

Sarmiento must have been impressed by the neat homes of the villages in the United States because he was accustomed to seeing very different types of dwellings, which are still in use today in practically all of South America, dwellings fashioned out of hand made mud bricks. He noted the kitchens of the homes and their utensils, the farm implements, stored in covered sheds, the shining harness, the ax, which he said is to the Yankee what the trunk is to the elephant, his toothpick and his finger, and the coaches, the machinery used for shelling corn and cleaning wheat and the neat gardens surrounded by white painted fences. All of this in a poor village of not even a dozen houses, hundreds of miles from the great cities and still surrounded by uncleared forests. He also describes the public establishments, the brewery, the bakery, the taverns, the hotels, the post office, the streets and their wide sidewalks shaded by rows of trees. The streets, until they are paved, were not so picturesque because the village pigs rooted in them, but Sarmiento explains that the pork products of the United States compete in importance with the products from the cultivation of wheat and therefore no one questions the pig his citizenship. Another sight which pleased Sarmiento in the small villages was the quality of workmanship and art in the beautifully executed signs. Throughout the United States, Sarmiento says, advertisements are works of art and are the most unmistakable evidence of the progress of the country.

I have had fun in Spain and all of South America examining those signs, wherever there are any, made with skinny hunch-backed letters and displaying with spelling errors the utmost ignorance of the worker or enthusiast who made them. The North American is a literary classicist in matters of advertise-ments, and a crooked or thick letter, or a mistake in spelling, would find the shopkeeper's counter deserted. (V, 355-356)

Sarmiento describes the villager's costume, saying that it

doesn't matter whether he is a tavernkeeper, a storekeeper or of other sedentary occupation, he daily wears patent leather boots, trousers and coat of black cloth, a black satin waistcoat, a cravat of heavy silk, a small cloth cap, and hanging from a black cord, a gold charm in the shape of a pencil or a key and at the end of the cord, a most curious part of the Yankee's costume, a watch which may be in any one of many varied sizes or shapes, "You will see fossilized watches, mastodon watches, ghostly watches, small insect-nest watches, three-story watches, inflated, with a draw-bridge and secret stairway, watches that you can wind only by descending to them with a lantern." (V, 356) He says that each boat that lands from Europe brings hundreds of these watches to meet the national popular demand for watches from three dollars up. Another fact of interest for Sarmiento was the habit of the Yankee of carrying a notebook for jotting down his plans for the next day.

Sarmiento says that if there is any thought that he has exaggerated the widespread evidence of civilization in the villages, in the cities and among all classes of the population, he will choose at random the smallest villages that he has a description of, and cites Pennington, with a town hall, a church, two academies, a bank and nearly three hundred inhabitants; Norwich, with several churches, a bank and seven hundred inhabitants; and Haverhill, a town hall, a bank, a church, an academy and sixty houses. West-ward, where civilization declines and is almost nonexistent because of the sparseness of the population, the aspect changes. There, comfort is reduced to a bare minimum and houses are mere log cabins, built in twenty-four hours out of logs set one on top of the other and crossed and dove-tailed at the corners.

But even in these remote plantations there is a perfect equality in the population, dress, manners, and even intel-ligence; the merchant, doctor, sheriff, farmer all look the same. The farmer is a family man, owner of two hundred or two thousand acres, which makes no difference in any event. His plowing instruments and engines are the same, that is, the best known; and if there happens to be a religious meeting in the vicinity, from the depth of the forests, coming down from the mountains, appearing on every road, you see farmers on horseback in big groups, with their black dress coats and trousers and the girls wearing the coolest materials in the prettiest patterns. (V, 357)

That differences of wealth and civilization were not expressed by special types of clothing, as in his country, pleased Sarmiento. He says that the Americans wear a common type of clothes and they even have a common bluntness of manner that preserves the appearance of equality in education.

But not even this is the greatest characteristic of that nation. It is their aptitude for appropriating, generalizing, vulgarizing, conserving and improving all customs, instruments, procedures and aids that the most advanced civilization has put in the hands of man. In this the United States is unique on earth. There is no invincible routine that delays for centuries the adoption of a known improvement. On the contrary, there is a predisposition to adopt everything. The advertisement made by a newspaper of a modification in the plow, for example, is copied in one day by all the newspapers in the Union. The next day this is talked about in all the plantations, and ironsmiths and manufacturers in two hundred places of the Union have tried out the model and made wagers on the sale of the new machines. At the same time a year later it is put in use throughout the Union. Just try to cause or hope for such a thing in a century in Spain, France or our [South] America. (V, 358)

Travel Facilities

Next after the villages, Sarmiento says that the attention of the visitor to the United States is drawn to the traffic on the wagon roads, the macadamized roads, the railroads or the canals that connect them. He says that if God were suddenly to call the world to judgment, he would surprise two-thirds of the American population on the road like ants. He says that since there is so much travel, no enterprise connected with travel is unprofitable. He gives the fares for the train from Albany to Buffalo, a distance of 360 miles, traveled in 24 hours for $12 and the steamboat fare from Cincinnati to New Orleans along the Ohio and Mississippi rivers, a distance of some 2,220 miles, with four sumptuous meals for ten days for $15. He says that the large number of passengers reduce the fares and the low fares in turn tempt the people to travel, even with no object in view other than just to enjoy a change of air or take a trip. He describes the trains as comfortable and roomy, even if the cushions are not so soft as the first-class coaches of France, nor as hard as the second-class cars in England, and since there is only one class of society in the United States — man — there is no need for several classes of coaches as in Europe. But he observes that where the North American luxury and greatness shows itself unrivaled on earth is in the steamboats on its northern rivers. Beside them, the boats of the Mediterranean look like row boats or cockle shells. He calls the steamboats three-story floating palaces, with many galleries and a promenade deck on the roof. He describes the *Isaac Newton* as having large richly decorated halls capable of holding the entire Senate and House of Representatives. Artistically draped damask hangings hide staterooms for fifteen hundred passengers, with colossal dining rooms with endless polished mahogany tables and procelain and silver service for a thousand guests. He also describes the *Hendrick* which travels from New York to Troy and Albany, a distance of 144 miles, and which has a capacity for 2000 passengers, for one dollar.

The South American who has just landed from Europe where he has delighted in admiring the progress of industry and the power of man, wonders in astonishment, when he sees those colossal American buildings, those facilities for locomotion, if Europe is really the leader in world civilization! I have seen French, English and Sardinian sailors express openly their amazement at finding themselves so small, so far behind this gigantic people. (V, 360)

Another interesting custom noted by Sarmiento was the special staterooms for the newly-wed couples on the steamboats on the Hudson. He says that Paris factories have created no curtains too costly for the gilded canopies of the bridal suites.

Stained glass windows cast the faint light that enters there with all the soft colors of the rainbow; rosy lamps burn at night; and by day and night the perfume of flowers, the fragrant waters and the aromas that are burning quench the thirst for pleasure that consumes their chosen occupants. (V, 361)

Marriage and Courtship Customs

Speaking of the bridal suites on the Hudson River steamboats, gave Sarmiento the opportunity to express himself about the marriage customs of the United States. He says that the Americans have developed customs unparalleled and unprecedented on earth.

The single woman is free as a butterfly until the moment of seclusion in the domestic cocoon, to fulfill her social functions in matrimony. Until that time she travels alone, wanders through city streets and has chaste free and easy love affairs in public, under the indifferent eye of her parents. She receives visits from persons who have not introduced themselves to her family and at two A.M. comes home from a dance accompanied by the man with whom she has danced exclusively a waltz or polka all evening. Her good Puritan parents tease her sometimes about the fellow, whose courtship they have heard about through gossip. And the sly girl takes pleasure in destroying conjecture by denying the evidence.

After two or three years of flirting, this is the North American word, of dances, promenades, trips and coquetries, the heroine of our story at lunch, like someone who does not like the situation, asks her parents if they know a tall, blond mechanic by trade who comes to see her from time to time, every day. They had been awaiting this introduction for a year. The solution is that there is a wedding agreed upon in the family, announced to the parents, who already knew about it from all the gossips in the neighborhood, on the day before. Once the wedding ceremony is over, the bride and groom set out in the first train to show their happiness, through the woods, towns, cities and hotels. On train coaches you always see these charming young twenty-year-old couples embracing, leaning on each other, and lavishing such expressive carresses that they edify all onlookers, causing even the most obstinate bachelors or old maids to decide to get married immediately. One cannot make propaganda for marriage in more insinuating terms that in this free exposition of married bliss. (V, 360-361)

Sarmiento says that no Yankee reaches the age of twenty-five without having a large family and that it is for this reason that the population of the United States has increased so rapidly. He cites the figures of the population in 1790 as 4,000,000, 1810 as 7,000,000, 1820 as 9,000,000, 1830 as 12,000,000, 1840 as 17,000,000 and in 1850 it is estimated to arrive at 23,000,000. While immigration has some bearing on these figures, it is of no great importance, Sarmiento says, and adds that the immigrant is not a prolific animal until he has had the Yankee bath.

Sarmiento then discusses the American marriage. After visiting Niagara Falls, bathing in the hot springs at Saratoga, and traveling three thousand miles in two weeks, the newly-weds return home

exhausted, full of wonder and happy, to become very bored in the home. The woman has said farewell forever to the world whose pleasures she enjoyed for so long a time with complete freedom; to the cool woods that witnessed her loves, to the cascade, the roads and rivers. In the future the close domestic shelter is her penitentiary forever, the roast beef her eternal accuser; the swarm of romping, blond children her constant torment, and a rude although good--natured husband perspiring in the daytime and snoring at night, her accomplice and spectre. (V, 362)

Continuing his impressions of the American, Sarmiento says that he is a born traveler and that the rage for traveling is increasing year by year, that the total revenue from public works, railroads, bridges, and canals in all the states in 1844, compared with those of the previous year, showed an increase of $4,000,000, which indicated a capital value of $80,000,000 in that year alone. He says that the American knows all the distances by heart and when approaching a city, he reaches for his wallet and unfolds a topographical map of the vicinity in order to locate the city in question. He compares the figure of 1,500,000 maps and atlases sold in the last ten years by a New York firm and declares that it is certain that no company in Paris has ever printed so many for sale all over the world. He says that no sooner had the Mexican war broken out than the Union was flooded with topographical maps of Mexico and the Yankees were able to follow the movements of the American army and adds that the Yankee wood choppers know more about Mexico in the topography, products, and natural resources than the Mexicans themselves.

Sarmiento describes the sights along the roads, saying that along scarcely passable roads leading out of the virgin forest, one can see a whole family with the ladies in ball dress, and the gentlemen in their eternal black coats in carriages just like those used in Washington. He says that the horses in their shining harness are of an English breed which has lost nothing of its slender Arab beauty in emmigrating to the New World, and he takes another dig at his forebears.

because the North American, far from barbarizing as we do the elements that European civilization handed down to us when it established colonies, works to improve them even more and open new pathways for them. (V. 363)

One might wonder what effect this would have upon Sarmiento. He had been traveling in the Old World and had seen all kinds of classes of society and kinds of governments. How would he react upon seeing in the United States that which was so different from all the rest he had seen.

The sight of this uniform decency and that general well-being, although it satisfies the hearts of those who observe a part of the human race, master in proportions common to all, of the pleasures and advantages of association, finally makes the eyes weary because of its monotonous uniformity; sometimes the appearance of a farmer with untidy clothes, dirty, faded jacket or ragged dress coat, enlivens the dull picture, which brings to the mind of the traveler the memory of Spanish or South American beggars whose appearance is so unpleasant. (V, 362)

Hotel St. Charles

Sarmiento describes the approach to New Orleans and the first glimpse of the cupola of the St. Charles hotel. The landscape was aglow with the autumn colors of the trees, below which were the emerald green lines of the sugar cane. Sarmiento says that although the surrounding countryside did not favor the comparison, the sight of the distant cupola reminded him of St. Peter's in Rome. He says that at last he was to see the United States a basilica worthy of the Christian cult. When someone asked him in what hotel he was planning to stop and recommended the St. Charles saying that from its cupola at sunrise the panorama of the city, river, lake and surrounding country was the finest, Sarmiento learned that the cupola which had so impressed him by its classical architecture and dimensions was merely a hotel.

Here is the regal people that builds palaces for itself to rest its head beneath its vaulted ceilings at night; here is tribute offered to man, inasmuch as he is man, and the wonders of art used to glorify the popular masses. (V, 365)

He continues in his description of the St. Charles hotel saying that there is no civil or religious monument in the United States, except the Capitol at Washington, which surpasses it, either in dimensions or good taste. He says that the interior of the building is as luxurious as its colossal exterior and notes that the lobby was filled with tables covered with newspapers from all over the United States as well as European ones of two weeks ago. He says that his traveling companion, who had previously shown himself all but indifferent to the advantages of this or any other system of government, after walking down street-like corridors leading to hundreds of bedrooms decorated with all the gradations of luxury said:

I am convinced through the intercession of St. Charles; now I believe in the republic, in democracy, in everything; I forgive the Puritans, even the one who ate raw tomato sauce with the tip of his knife and before his soup. Everything, however, should be forgiven the people who erect monuments to the dining room and crown the kitchen with a cupola like this. (V, 366)

Notwithstanding the fact that the St. Charles hotel cost $700,000, Sarmiento says that it is neither the largest nor the best constructed of the popular palaces. Every large city boasts two or three magnificent hotels, that vie with each other in serving the public at very low prices. He says that no more money has been spent on any of the many churches in New York than on the Astor Hotel in Washington Square, New York. Sarmiento in-

terprets the role of the hotel in the life of the nation and believes
that it is significant that the hotels of the United States are so
important.

Since I have visited the United States and have seen the
results obtained there spontaneously, I have a strange
procupation, which is that in order to find out whether a
machine, invention or social doctrine is useful and applicable
or good for future development, one must test the corner-
stone of the spontaneous application of the Yankees. Today
hotels play an important part in the domestic life of nations.
Stationary nations, like Spain and its descendants, do not
need hotels; for them their home is sufficient. In the busy
towns, with life present and future, the hotel will be above
any other public building. (V, 367)

Eating Customs

Sarmiento describes the breakfast hour in the hotel, saying
that at half past seven in the morning the hideous din of a Chinese
gong sounds through all the corridors to advise the guests that the
rising hour has arrived, and again at eight to announce that breakfast is ready. Then the crowd of guests rushes to the immense
dining room. Here the life of these people, as serious when they
laugh as when they eat, begins to be seen. And in a society where
all men, down to the last individual are equal, there is no protection for the weak nor rank to set apart the powerful. Sarmiento
says it would be sad for the women if the hotel regulations did not
come to their rescue, giving them the privilege of being seated
first, along with their husbands and relatives, and the un-
accompanied men only when the gong was sounded. When the
gong sounds, there is instantly such a din of noise with chairs
scraping across the floor, plates, knives and forks striking against
each other that it is possible to be a half a league away and know
that eating has begun.

It is impossible to view the evolutions that happen in that
hubbub, despite the activity and skill of fifty or a hundred
servants who try to give a certain rhythmic order as they
uncover the food or pour tea or coffee. The North American
has set aside two minutes for lunch, five for dinner, ten for

smoking or chewing tobacco, and all his free moments for casting a glance at the newspaper which you are reading, the only newspaper that interests him because another person is already busy reading it. (V, 370)

The four regular meals are breakfast, lunch, dinner and tea although breakfast may be served at five o'clock in the morning for those who have to travel at that hour. Nor is a meal ever begrudged to new guests, no matter the hour of arrival. Then Sarmiento describes his horror at the manner of eating.

And then, what inconsistencies! What incest and promiscuity in the food! The pure-blooded Yankee serves himself on the same plate, together or in succession, all the food, desserts and fruits. We have seen one from the Far West, a land of doubtful location, like the Ophir of the Phoenicians, who would begin his meal with fresh tomato sauce, taken in huge quantity, by itself and with the tip of his knife! Sweet potatoes with vinegar! (V, 370)

Manners

Sarmiento had other observations to make about the question of manners. He found that in the reading rooms, four or five pushing fellows will lean heavily over your shoulder to read what you are trying to read. If you are going down stairs, or through a door, the person behind you will invariably jostle you. If you are quietly smoking, a passer-by will snatch your cigar out of your mouth to light his own, and then put it back again. If you are reading a book and look up, your neighbor will appropriate it and read two chapters. If you happen to have unusual buttons on your vest, such as a deer, horse, or boar's head in relief, everyone who notices them will come up to examine them, turning each one from right to left and from left to right so as to inspect your traveling museum. If you wear a full beard in the north, it is a sign that you are French or Polish, and you will find yourself at every step the center of attention by a circle of men who will gaze at you with childish inquisitiveness and invite their friends and acquaintances to step up and satisfy their curiosity. Of course it is understood that you may take all of these liberties with other people without giving rise to any complaints or in any way appearing to be disagreeable. Sarmiento continues in his observations of the manners, saying that the height of genius is the way the nation pays constant veneration to its feet — that while conversing with you, the Yankee of careful breeding will rest one foot on his knee, remove his shoe to rub his foot, and listen to whatever complaints his overworked toes may have to make. Furthermore, four persons seated at a marble topped table will invariably rest their eight feet on it, unless they can find a chair upholstered in velvet. He describes the manner of sitting in chairs, which he observed once in the Tremont Hotel in Boston, saying that two were seated with their feet on the table, one with his feet resting on the cushion of a nearby chair, another with a leg hooked over the arm of his own chair, another with both heels on the edge of the cushion of his chair so as to prop his chin on his two knees, and another embracing the back of his chair with his leg in the same way as one is accustomed to put his arms. Sarmiento didn't remember having seen anyone sitting on the back of the chair and putting his feet in the cushion but that he is certain that he has seen no one who prided himself on courtesy in the natural posture. Lying down is the height of elegance, and Sarmiento caustically says that people in the know reserve this gesture of good breeding for times when ladies are present or when listening to the speech of the opposition in Congress.

Sarmiento admired the characteristic of the Yankee who never had a discussion in matters of religion and politics except with those of the same opinion or sect. He says that this admirable and conciliatory doctrine is based upon a thorough understanding of human nature. The Yankee orator tries to confirm his adherents in their beliefs, rather than to persuade his opponents — who are meanwhile sleeping or ruminating about their own affairs — of the error of their views. But the Yankee is the most uncivil brute under the sun, according to the views of such competent judges as Captain Marryat, Mrs. Trollope and other travelers. But Sarmiento defends the Americans, saying that if coal miners, wood choppers and firemen were to sit down at the table in France or England with artists, deputies, bankers, and landowners, as happens in the United States, the Europeans would have a different opinion about their own culture.

In cultured countries good manners have their natural limits. The English lord is uncivil because of pride and scorn for his inferiors, while the majority are rude due to stupidity and ignorance. In the United States civilization is practiced upon such a large mass of people that the purifying is done slowly; the influence of the rough masses acts on the individual and forces him to adopt the customs of the majority, finally creating a sort of national taste which causes pride and concern. The Europeans poke fun at the more apparent than real rude habits and the Yankees in a spirit of contradiction persist in them and pretend to place them under the banner of freedom and the American spirit. Without favoring these habits nor insisting upon excusing them, after having traveled about the principal nations of the Christian world, I am convinced that North Americans are the only cultured people on earth, the ultimate result attained by modern civilization. (V, 372-373)

Sarmiento says that the Europeans and South Americans find fault with the Yankees for many defects of character, but that he respects these very defects, which he attributes to the whole human race, to our times, to hereditary preoccupations, and to the imperfections of our minds.

A nation composed of all the peoples of the world, free as conscience, as the air, without guardians, armies, limits, the result of all European and Christian ancestors. Their defects should, then, be those of the human race in a given period of development. But as a nation, the United States is the final result of human logic. It has no kings, nobles, privileged classes, men born to rule nor human machines born to obey. Is this result not in conformity with the ideas of justice and equality that Christianity accepts theoretically? Wealth is distributed more widely than in any nation. The population grows according to laws unknown up to now among other nations; production goes on with astonishing progress. Can it be, as the Europeans claim, that none of this enters into freedom of action and lack of government? (V, 374)

Reasons for Wealth and Prosperity

Sarmiento declares that if all this prosperity is due to the settling of a new land, as the Europeans assert, why then in South

America, where it is even easier to take up new land, is neither wealth nor population on the increase. He asks why in the cities and even the capitals there have not been built even a hundred new houses during the past ten years. He says that no census has yet been taken of the mental capacity of any nation, that population is counted by noses and from such figures, the strength and capacity of a nation are computed. Sarmiento says that for war such data might be of interest but that in the case of the Americans, there is one peculiarity that invalidates the figure, because, he says, one Yankee is worth many of other nationalities for killing men, declaring that the destructive capacity of the United States might be estimated at two hundred million. He cites as proof the fact that the rifle is the national weapon, target practice is the sport of children in the forest states and the practice of hunting squirrels by shooting their feet off, in order not to ruin the pelt, produces an astonishing skill which is universal. (How would Sarmiento estimate the destructive capacity of the United States a hundred years later — with atomic bombs, instead of rifles?)

More impressed was Sarmiento by the statistics which showed that the number of adult males corresponds to a population of twenty million inhabitants — all educated, able to read and write, and enjoying political rights, with exceptions that do not change the situation in general. More than that, Sarmiento says that the American male is a man with a home or with the certainty of owning one, beyond the reach of hunger and despair, able to hope for any future that his imagination is capable of conjuring up. "Man, finally master of himself, his spirit raised by education and the feeling of his dignity." (V, 375) Sarmiento says that it is believed that man is a rational being in that he is able to acquire and exercise reason; and in this sense, no country in the world possesses a greater number of rational beings, even though it might have ten times the population of the United States.

Psychology of the People

To demonstrate the difference in the psychology of the people, Sarmiento describes the French and American railroads, saying that the French system is so well planned and calculated and checked that the train does not leave the platform until four minutes after an army of guards has ascertained that every traveler is in his seat, all doors are closed, the road is free, and no one within a yard of where the train will pass. Wooden fences guard both sides of the right of way, double tracks of cast-iron rails facilitate traffic in either direction and if a local road crosses the track, strong gates guard the crossing, which is closed a quarter of an hour before the train is due, in order to avoid accidents. Along side of this picture of protection, Sarmiento describes the railroads in the United States, which pass through miles of primeval forest, with no human habitation, on a single track laid upon wooden rails, with sidings constructed at intervals so that the trains may pass, with only a sign at the country crossings warning one to listen for the bell before crossing, with tracks running through villages, and children standing at their front doors to wait for the train to pass, or in the middle of the roadbed. The train starts slowly and when it is already in motion, one can see the passengers jumping aboard and the fruit and newspaper venders hopping off, for amusement or for the feeling of their freedom.

> The physical and moral results of both systems are too obvious. Europe with its ancient learning and wealth accumulated for centuries, has not been able to open half of the railroads that facilitate movement in North America. The European is a minor under the protective guardianship of the state; his instinct of preservation is not reputed to be sufficiently preservative. Iron gratings, doors, vigilantes, warning signs, inspection, safety locks have all been put into practice to protect life: everything but reason, discernment, fearlessness, freedom; everything but his right to take care of himself, his intentions and his will. The Yankee takes care of himself and if he wants to kill himself nobody will stop him; if he runs after the train to catch it, if he dares to jump and grab on to the bar, jumping over the wheels, he is free to do so. If the naughty little newspaper boy, wanting to sell one more copy, has let the train start full force, and jumps off, everybody applauds the skill with which he has jumped, stood up, and continues on his way on foot. This is how the character of nations is formed and how liberty is practiced. Perhaps there are a few more victims and accidents, but on the other hand, there are free men and not disciplined prisoners to whom life is administered. (V, 378)

Sarmiento noted that the word "passport" was unknown in the United States and that the Yankee who comes across one of those European documents wherein the movements of the traveler are inscribed, is horrified. The child who wishes to take a train, steamboat or canal boat, Sarmiento says, will have no one to question him. Nor the unmarried girl who wants to go on a six hundred mile trip.

They use their liberty and right to move about. Consequently the Yankee child amazes the European because of his self--assurance, cautious prudence, and his knowledge of life at the age of ten. (V, 379)

Yankee Ships

Another source of admiration for Sarmiento was the Yankee ship, which he said was the best, the cheapest and the largest in the world. He says that in European ports and docks you can see a special section where these colossal ships are moored and that they seem to belong to another world and to other men. He praised the fact that schedules were kept, no matter what the weather might be and says that if on a stormy day you see a ship insisting on sailing, you can be sure that it is a Yankee ship whose departure has been posted for that day and no amount of wind or weather would postpone its sailing. Sarmiento also admired the solitary crews who hunted whales in the polar seas, saying that they were men inured to hardship, who snatch a tidy fortune from the jaws of death to set themselves up on their return to the United States with the purchase of a piece of land to clear and build a house. He says that almost invariably they are Americans and they drink nothing alcoholic since they are members of the Temperance Society. He says he puts especial emphasis upon this matter of the United States marine, because the nation which has the swiftest ships — those of cheapest construction and therefore of lowest freight rates — is king of the universe. Sarmiento felt that the fact that American ships were superior was a result of the God-given resources of the United States, along with democracy.

God has willed finally that there be brought together in one single deed, in one nation, the virgin land that allows society to expand infinitely without fear of poverty, iron that adds to human strength, coal that activates machines, forests that provide materials for naval architecture, popular education which through general education strengthens the force of production in all the individuals of a nation, religious freedom which attracts people in masses to become part of the population, political liberty which looks with horror on despotism and privileged families, in fact, the strong republic rising like a new star in the sky. And all these facts bring together freedom and abundant land, iron and industrial genius, democracy and the superiority of ships. Persist in separating them by theories and speculation, say that liberty and popular education have nothing to do with this extraordinary prosperity which leads inevitably to an indisputable supremacy. The fact will always remain the same, that in European monarchies a large amount of decrepitude, revolutions, poverty, ignorance, barbarity and degradation have come together. (V, 401)

Stability of the Republic

Sarmiento added that meanwhile a half a million soldiers are needed to keep in equilibrium the jealousy and envy of one monarch for another, the republic works like a beehive, saves immense sums of money which it turns into stepping-stones to prosperity, power and strength. He says that the science and study of the monarchies are not used by them but rather by the republic, where it serves to increase its splendor. He recalls that Franklin had the temerity to appear in the most ostentatious court in the world dressed in coarse clothes and hobnailed boots and warns the monarchies that someday they will be forced to hide their scepters, crowns, and gilded baubles before presenting themselves before the republic, for fear that it may show them the door, like comedians or buffoons at carnival time.

Moral and Ethical Character

Sarmiento discusses the moral character of the United States and says that the United States as a government is irreproachable in its public acts but that the individuals who make up the population suffer from repugnant vices. He asks the reason for such a condition, asking if such is a characteristic of the Anglo-saxon

race, or is the result of the mixture of so many different races, or
whether it is the thankless fruit of liberty and democracy.

Do not be astonished if I point out that I attribute the moral
evil that afflicts those peoples to this last reason, more than
to any other. Greed is the legitimate daughter of liberty itself. It is there that the human species shows itself, without
any disguise, just as it is, in the period of civilization it has
reached and as will be demonstrated for still more centuries,
while the profound revolution which the United States leads
and which is taking place in human destinies, comes to an
end. (V, 403)

It is Sarmiento's opinion that with the changing world, the
ideas of ethics change also. No one is scandalized by the fact that
steam has been applied to locomotion, nor that electricity is used
for the transmission of words. In a like manner, he says, the
United States has added a new concept of the system of ethics in
relation to democracy. Meanwhile the ancient and modern
moralists have all followed the idea that poverty and suffering of
the masses is unavoidable or even necessary, and must be accepted
by the poor with resignation along with a little charity of the rich;
Franklin has proclaimed well-being along with virtue; be righteous
in order to obtain more, obtain more in order to be righteous.
Sarmiento says that Franklin was very much like Moses in his
principles of ethics and that all modern laws are based on this new
idea of ethics, of opening the door to comfort and riches to the
masses. And it is for this reason that the entire energy of the
people in the United States is engaged in accumulating capital to
establish themselves and that they are so accustomed to struggle
for that which they covet, that they may depart from the ethical if
it is a hindrance to their objective. Sarmiento says that the people
of the United States, in mass, are not very ethical as yet and is
disguised by the common appearance which each has with the
other. In any other part of the world, he says you can tell just by
looking at a person whether he is a farmer, a beggar, a priest, a
salesman or a tramp, but in the United States all men at first sight
are alike — just men. It is for this reason that liberty and equality
produce moral defects, which are not so evident in other parts,
because the majority of the others are incapable of showing them.
They are more evident in the United States because of the organi-

zation of the country. Sarmiento says that there is such a feeling of life experienced in the United States, so much confidence in the future, so much faith in the results of labor, so great the possibilities that credit lies in the individual rather than in the guarantee of property.

He cites the fact that even some states have been guilty of repudiating their debts contracted in building new railroads or canals, but that later when other states have shown a reaction against such as a national disgrace, the guilty ones have settled their obligations, being moved by ideas of honor. Sarmiento says that the state, which remains inert in defiance of universal law, is very poor, very distant and very ignorant.

Another grave defect that Sarmiento notes is the application of the lynch law, which he calls a civil crime. He says that in the far-west or in the slave states, wherever there happen to be seven men together, they take the matter of justice in their own hands. "You will be hanged by those judges, more terrible and arbitrary than the invisible judges of the secret tribunals of ancient Germany." (V, 411)

Declared the defects, Sarmiento points out the civilizing currents which carry the ideas of improvement, light and moral progress to the farthermost corners of the United States. He recalls the early colonists of the original thirteen colonies, the Pilgrims in New England, the Quakers in Pennsylvania and the Catholics in Maryland and says that such colonization was not so much of men but rather of political ideas and religious ideas, in search of air and space for growth. Their fruits were the Declaration of Independence in 1776, which Sarmiento says is the first page of the history of the modern world and of all the political revolutions which will follow.

In the expansion of the United States, Sarmiento points out that the older states engender the new ones. The Indian hater goes first into the wilderness to rout the Indians from their hunting grounds, then comes the squatter, who enjoys the wide open spaces and the clearing of the new lands, and finally the pioneer, who cultivates the land. Then come the contractors with their foreign laborers to build the cities and lay the railroads. Following this scheme, the youth of the older states come in search of their fortune, and set up businesses. In this expansion of the population, various grades of civilization are seen, and almost disappear in the west, where the people are most scattered and also for reason of the crude occupations, as well as in the south for the existence of slaves along with the Spanish and French traditions. Sarmiento reminds us that there the immigrant element is poor, ignorant and generally not accustomed to democratic practices but asks how to proceed in order to transform this mass of immigrants into citizens who will feel a part of the order. He says that one of the most effective means is the daily newspaper which contains some topic of conversation about the news of the Union. Another of the important influences is the election of the president.

The election of the president is the only link that joins all the borders of the Union, the only national concern that at one time moves all men and all states. The electoral struggle is therefore an awakener, a school and stimulant which revives life that has been dormant because of distances and the harshness of work. (V, 412)

Religion and Religious Tolerance

But the greatest influence of all is the religious feeling. Sarmiento says that for a lukewarm South American Catholic it is astonishing to see the high and extensive scale upon which religion operates in the midst of that extreme North American liberty. He remarked about the reading of the Bible, and says that for good or evil, the Bible is read daily over the country — from the log cabin to the hotels of the great cities. Controversies between the sects give greater interest to this reading and there are some seventy-four theological schools throughout the nation; meanwhile there are only ten for the study of law. Sarmiento says that there are three times as many original works about religious science as there are about scientific investigations. He describes the itinerant pastors who spend their lives traveling through the back country to keep the sacred fires alive.

Rough and energetic men who take activity everywhere awaken spirits, arousing them to the contemplation of eternal truths. These are true spiritual exercises like those of Catholics, even more spiritual, for without intimidating them with the punishments of hell, the pastor or pastors gathered at a religious meeting outdoors or in some improvised shed, shake up the dull minds of the country folk, present to them

the image of God in inconceivably grandiose terms; and when
the stimulus has produced its effect, they send the women
into the woods on one side and the men on the other, so that
they can meditate alone, and find themselves in their own
presence, seeing their own nothingness, helplessness and
moral defects. (V, 413-414)

He then describes the strange effects of these religious
exercises. Such practices still exist today in certain parts of the
country among the "Holy Rollers."

The results of this moral cure are strange and unexplainable.
The women go into their trances, twist and roll on the floor,
frothing at the mouth; the men cry and clench their fists
until finally a religious hymn sung in chorus slowly begins to
sweeten their holy sorrows, reason takes command, conscience is pacified and calmed, and a deep melancholy is cast
over their faces, mixed with symptoms of moral goodness as
if the feeling of righteousness had been strengthened with
that emetic applied to the soul. (V, 414)

One more civilizing factor, Sarmiento says, must be
mentioned, the one most active in keeping American religious,
political and industrial life full of the old colonial spirit, and
accessible to every progressive achievement of the modern mind —
the inhabitant of New England, the descendant of the ancient
Pilgrims, the heir to their tradition of resignation and hard, manual
labor, and the elaborator of the great moral and social ideas that
make up the American nationality. He compares them to the
Brahmins, saying that they have spread over the western part of
the United States, educating by their example and skill the new
and untrained peoples. He says we must not forget that the
Pilgrims were a hundred and fifty wise, thoughtful, fanatical,
enthusiastic, politically minded immigrants, tested by every
calamity that men can experience and that today the descendants
of that select group of humanity are the mentors and leaders of
the new generations.

It is believed that more than one million families in the whole
Union are descended from that noble stock. They have
imprinted upon the face of the Yankee that placid kindliness

which is noticeable in the better educated class. They take to all the Union a manual skill that makes North America a walking arsenal of workmen, with an iron-like energy to struggle with difficulties and overcome them, and the moral and intellectual aptitude which places them on a level with the best of the human race, if not a higher one. These immigrants of the north discipline the new arrivals, inject their spirit into them at the meetings they promote and preside over, in schools, books, elections and in the practice of all North American institutions. They initiate and carry out the great enterprises of colonization and railroads, of banks and societies. (V, 415-416)

Thus it is, he says, that the incivility produced by the isolation of the forests and the relaxation of democratic practices introduced by the immigrants is checked by the influence of the Pilgrims, because in the ebb and flow of the two opposite forces is the mixture of the position of the races and the end result is that the new elements take on a homogeneity which preserves the original type, the traditional and progressive characteristics which distinguish the descendants of the Pilgrims. Sarmiento asks whether such a thing happens in the rest of the world in such a notable and constant manner.

Sarmiento admired the religious tolerance found in the United States even though he was astounded by the many sects. He believed that the time would come when the citizens of the United States would present to the world the demonstration of a people universally devout, but without an apparent religious form similar to the situation in China, where there is a religion but no cult, but where the population practice the teachings of Confucius. Sarmiento says that if such happens, and he believes it ought to happen, how wonderful and fruitful it will be for humanity to have experienced such an event, which will result in dignifying man, in elevating the human moral and add to the well being of all the achievements of the human intelligence. "That the North American is the beginning of religious tolerance is inscribed in all its constitutions and has become a popular saying." (V, 419)

Temperance Societies

Sarmiento was impressed with the campaign against drunkenness, saying that there are thousands of Temperance Society members who have pledged not to touch alcoholic drinks so that the world may be cured of this disease which ruins all economy and destroys all morals. He praises the generosity of the North American in giving a part of his income for the propagation of religious ideas, and for missionary work in other countries. He notes the establishment of schools with money left by rich men and says that in all this complicated work one will see predominate one grand idea, that of equality, which is a religious feeling that the soul is the basis of the individual and national existence.

Elections

Sarmiento remarks that there were two things he was very interested in seeing first hand in the United States, the way the desert is populated and the manner of holding elections. He says that he has observed the system of colonizing, and even though it might appear to be without science, nevertheless, there is a system of principles, rules and laws. He says that the Spanish colonization of South America is the cause of many of its problems and that he has information to prepare a study which will fill a great need among the South American countries. As for elections, he says that he was able to see only one election, that of mayor in Baltimore. He says that the system of elections is a new idea recently germinated and that only in the United States has it developed sufficiently to be practical. The only election incident he saw was the effort of the Democratic newspapers to convince the Irish immigrants to vote for the Democrats instead of the Whigs. He was not very edified with this demonstration, since the Irish immigrant in the United States would correspond to the penniless in Chile, and neither has much knowledge of what would be the best for the country. Since he was not able to witness or study the system of elections, he quotes at length from Combe about the elections in the United States and gives an impartial description of the elections in various of large cities.

Conclusion

Sarmiento's stay in the United States lasted less than three months, but few have traveled so much or seen all that he did in

that time. He noted everything that he saw and thought of how it
might be applied to the countries he had left. It was not that he
wanted to make Yankees of the South Americans, but rather that
he felt that his countrymen could take advantage of the
experience realized by the new republic; and that with all its
defects, he was convinced that the United States was the most
advanced along the road to the promised land. He discovered in
the United States a new social world, different from that of
Europe and South America. He attributed the marvel that he
found there to the richness of the soil, hard work, education,
democratic institutions, religious tolerance and liberty of enterprise, ideal and thought.

> Their faith in the future of the United States was absolute
> because of the breath of cosmic life which encouraged the
> people. The land of America was their source of life, their
> medium, the individual valued for his capacity and work,
> their goal the fusion of different peoples into a new nation
> thanks to education and freedom.[1]

3. Influence upon Sarmiento

During the next forty years, or the rest of his life, Sarmiento
never stopped watching the United States in its progress. He saw
his prophecies fulfilled; the new social world continued its advance. Sarmiento had arrived at an age of mature judgment, and
because of his varied experiences and profound interest in human
welfare, he was able to evaluate the experiment he saw in the
United States. Thoroughly separated from Spain and disillusioned
with what he had seen in Europe, he rejoiced with the example
that he found in the United States. Here was what he had dreamed
of for years, and with the passing of time Sarmiento saw the new
orientation of South America, thanks to his unceasing efforts,
follow the path traced by the new republic of the north. Not that
the republic was perfect but to Sarmiento it appeared to have the
necessary ingredients for continued development and growth. He
saw the historic similarities of the Americas, European colonization, independence and federal organization and wanted also the
technical progress, the religious tolerance, education and freedom.
Sarmiento had been educated with French books of the
eighteenth century but with his studies, contacts with men and

governments, and his travels, he began to rebel against these teachers who educated South America in liberalism. In an unedited, undated, original manuscript in the Mitre Museum Sarmiento declares that he stopped being French when he returned from the United States and that with the publication of *Crónica y Sud América*, he began a complete change of his ideas. He says:

> Other variations enter into my ideas of the affairs of government as I see and contemplate results, travel, read, study and deal with men. I had been educated with French books, the eighteenth century, the revolution, the liberals of the time of Louis Philippe. In a letter of Tejedor about my travels I now find signs of my revolt against the authority of these masters of liberalism which I teach South America and communicate to it an inability to create a government in order to preserve that beloved liberty. . . . Since that day other ideas take hold, modifying the previous ones without destroying them. Lately on my return from the United States, having ceased to be French, I began in the *Crónica* and *South America*, publications in Chile, the complete change of face that I was seen to make.[2]

Political Influence

Sarmiento believed that it was necessary to establish a government to preserve the freedom which had been gained with independence. He says that after forty years of struggle and strife, it is not freedom which has not been able to establish itself in South America but rather the government, which has to preserve freedom.

> We in South America find memories of freedom neither in the colonies nor in the mother country, nor in the history of Spain, which as a nation begins with Queen Isabella busy robbing the Jews, expelling the Moors, and Charles V who puts an end to common liberties, in Philip II who lights the bonfires; and in spite of this, since the day the Independence revolution began, we find floating in the air the feeling of personal dignity of the individual, the desire for liberty, and in forty years of struggle we have acquired all the freedoms in

their useful aims. It is not liberty that could not be established in South America but the government that must protect it.[3]

In his letters to Mitre, Sarmiento often refers to his impressions of his trip to the United States. Thus we see him writing from Santiago, Chile, to Mitre in the year of the Argentine Constitution about his beliefs as to the form of government the country should take.

I am a Federalist by conviction. My travels and familiarity with North American institutions lead me to desire this form of government whenever that is possible. There is no republic in the world but that of the United States.[4]

In a letter written in June 1854 from Santiago, Sarmiento tells Mitre again,

And so, we must work to make the forms and institutions more closely related to those of North America.[5]

In a letter written from Yungay in January 1855, Sarmiento repeats to Mitre his ideas about using the United States as a model:

Industry, education, liberty, institutions, the future, all is there, and from there it is necessary to spread them over these countries . . . and the federation and institutions already proven in the United States by almost one century of success are going to be for the modern republic what Roman legislation has been for all modern peoples, that all have adopted. South America is going to be federal, Mexico will be too. New Granada (Colombia) has just made Panama a state and is going to continue organizing the others. . . . Europe is going to be federal.[6]

Nor were the ideas of government, industry, institutions, and education the only ones we see influencing Sarmiento's thinking after he had returned to Chile from the United States, for in a letter to Mitre written in April 1854 he writes about the need for statistics, for a census of the population and also of the cattle industry. He reminds Mitre that the United States at that time had twenty-eight million cattle, thirty-one million sheep, thirty million hogs, four million horses and half a million mules. Sarmiento believed that in order to make Argentina attractive for immigrants, it was necessary to be on the map with facts. Such deeds would speak for themselves and the country would grow.

Passports

Sarmiento noted the freedom with which the inhabitants of the United States travel without the use of a passport. He writes in *La Crónica* in March 1849 shortly after his return to Chile.

> The word *passport* does not exist in the United States and there are people who request this rare curiosity from those who come from Europe only to be amazed to see so many scribbles and signatures. There are one hundred and thirty-eight railroads, and the merchant closes his door, gets into a coach and twenty-four hours later is one hundred leagues away without anyone knowing where he came from or where he is going. He does the same with ships, and departs for Chile or Calcutta ten minutes after he had conceived the idea of leaving his country. This freedom of action is not detrimental to United States business. . . . There is no *passport* in England, the United States, Switzerland, where man is respected, where the real interests of commerce are understood; it consists of facilitating free freight without asking anyone if that movement is caused by legitimate or criminal motives, because there is no crime in moving. (X, 78-79)

Governments Role in Promoting Economy

Sarmiento believed that it was the duty of the government to encourage the individual in business by aiding him in the opening of canals, laying of railroads and shipping on the navigable rivers, with the object of cheapening the costs of transportation, all of which contributed to the prosperity of the nation. Furthermore, he pointed out the advantages of the governments activating correspondence in order to promote business. He said that in the United States the mail service carries correspondence, magazines, samples, money and passengers from one part to another, traveling 142,295 miles per day.

> It is a common fact that the wealth of a nation consists of the sum of the wealth of individuals who form that nation; and the concern of governments should be limited to making the means of getting rich easy for everyone. For example, England, France, the United States have opened great canals, by navigating rivers, have established railroads for the purpose of making production less costly so that each will spend less on transportation, that is, each proprietor will earn twenty-five percent that he would not have made if such routes had not been opened. The other protection the State gives is that of activating correspondence and assuring vigilance in communications, without which big mercantile negotiations cannot be made. (X, 89)

In November 1853 Sarmiento writes in *La Crónica* about agriculture in the United States, urging that such methods as used there be adopted in Argentina. He praises the work carried on by the U. S. Patent Office, especially in that of seed exchange with other countries.

> We must show how the government of the United States proceeds in this respect. In that huge laboratory of wealth there is not any county seat supported by the government. The whole country is a county seat where new plows, corn-husking, seeding or threshing machines are tested. The government through the Patent Office sends circulars every year to all parts of the Union asking what crops are thriving, what instruments are used, what fertilizers the soil requires, how much grain an acre of land produces, how much the job is worth and what use it permits. How much it costs to raise a horse, to what breed the parents of the colts belong, what breeds of cattle, pigs, lambs are bred, etc., and from these reports, which number more than three hundred, the government publishes a book of one hundred thousand copies which are distributed throughout the Union, taking useful knowledge, improvements, announcements, information to all parts of the country. (X, 225)

Education

Perhaps the greatest influence the United States had upon Sarmiento's thinking was the matter of education. He had been surprised to find the entire nation reading newspapers and he believed that the first prerequisite for a democracy was to educate the people, for he said that an ignorant people will always elect a Rosas. He had gone to Europe believing in the superiority of the schools he would find there, but after visiting the United States, he declared that its schools were the pedestal of democracy, and tells of the geologist Lyell, educated in the famous University of Oxford, inviting England to study science at Harvard University, which he admires as superior to all those of Europe.

Educación Popular and *Educación Común*, forming Volumes XI and XII of the complete works of Sarmiento, were written upon his return to Chile and contain excellent studies of the education systems observed by Sarmiento in Europe and in the United States with suggestions and recommendations for public education. Even though *Educación Popular* was written in 1849 and *Educacion Común* in 1855, they still may be read with interest by those interested in knowing how advanced Sarmiento was in his pedagogic ideas. Especially, it should be pointed out, Sarmiento pleaded for the education of women, saying that their education should not be treated as a mere adornment but rather as the key to the destiny of the nation. "On the education of women depends the fate of the United States; civilization stops at the doors of the home when women are not ready to receive it." (XI, 122)

Libraries

Along with the educational system of the United States, Sarmiento admired the libraries which provided a part of the education of the people. He said that even though there are larger and more valuable collections of books in Europe, they are of little value until they are made accessible to the public.

For it is clear that the treasures of the enormous Paris Library are of little use to the resident of Lyons if he does not take a trip to consult them. . . . With the general system of education there has begun in the United States (a theater of the application of the greatest rules of common sense) the formation of thousands of libraries which, without being as rich as the European ones, are more effective in developing the culture of a country, and the indispensable location of an adequate auxiliary library along with each educational establishment. Schools have them; secondary schools have larger and more complete libraries but no literary or political society lacks its special library. The primary schools of New York have ten thousand libraries and the one hundred-sixty private academies must give an account to the Regents of the University of the number and titles of the books they add to their collections. (XII, 134)

In *La Crónica* in December 1849, Sarmiento wrote about the need for books. He compared the educational conditions to the uncultivated lands, saying that for each hundred acres of cultivated land, there are a thousand acres neglected, and for each man who has cultivated his intelligence, there are ten thousand who are ruled only by animal passions and appetites. He declares that ideas are transmitted by education, by deeds and by books and asks what are the books which the public reads. He says that since the bookseller in Paris or Barcelona is interested in selling, it is difficult to find works of a serious nature; while there are thirty editions of *Misterios de Paris*, he asks if there is one of *De Democracia* by Tocqueville or *Historia de la civilización* by Guizot. He asks that the government try the same idea that was tried in France, England and the United States, of popularizing the classics and giving the people books in order to cultivate their minds.

Why wouldn't they try in Chile something similar that would result in spreading throughout the country within ten years, a mass of knowledge among a large number of readers? How many books on history, geography, travels, domestic arts, agriculture, politics could in this way circulate in the country and leave in the head of everyone who might read them, useful ideas, exact notions, varied knowledge! Two thousand copies of a book can mean twenty thousand readers and twenty thousand readers in Chile can be a lever of progress superior to the resistance of inertia. (VI, 345)

Conclusion

Thus we can deduce that the years that followed Sarmiento's visit to the United States were to be filled with fruitful work, as the years before had been; but now, he had a new model to imitate. Richard Rojas sums it up as follows:

It is not that I should like to make Yankees of us but that I was wishing for our peoples a destiny such as that of the Yankees, profiting from their experience achieved in stages analogous to ours: European colonization, republican emancipation, federal organization, assimilating immigration, technical progress, religious tolerance, education and freedom.[7]

Chapter II
SECOND VISIT TO THE UNITED STATES

1. Conditions in the United States

Sarmiento arrived in New York on the 15th of May, 1865 for his second visit in the United States. This time he came not as a sightseer but as the Ambassador of his country to the United States Government, where he would remain for more than three years. Much had happened in the eighteen years since his first visit. Upon his return to Chile he had married and gone to live in the home of his wife at Yungay, where he spent perhaps the most peaceful years of his stormy life. There he was to increase his literary fame with *Viajes, Educación popular, Recuerdos de provincia* and *Argiropolis*. Here he spent delightful hours with his son, Dominguito, the memories of which he would cherish always. In 1851 he and Mitre had left Chile to join in the army of General Urquiza to fight against Rosas. Following the victory at Caseros, Sarmiento again chose to return to Chile until 1855, when he tried to return to Argentina but when he arrived to Mendoza, he was arrested. So again he fled to Chile but the following year he went to Buenos Aires, where he was named superintendent of schools in 1857. In 1858 he was named senator from the Province of Buenos Aires, in 1860 he was named minister of interior by the government of Buenos Aires and shortly thereafter minister to the United States, but he resigned both when the war broke out again between the Province of Buenos Aires and the Argentine Confederation. Following the battle of Pavón in 1861, he went into the interior with General Paunero and in 1862 became governor of his Province, San Juan. In 1864 he was named as minister plenipotentiary to Chile, Peru and the United States. Thus we can observe that his life had not been idle during this interim of eighteen years.

Appointment as Minister

Sarmiento had wanted to return to the United States for some time. We learn in a letter written from Yungay, Chile, to Mitre on April 8th, 1854 that Sarmiento would prefer to go to the United States instead of returning to Buenos Aires,

> to study there matters of administration and education, the practice of federal and municipal institutions, the character and nature of liberty, the ways to generalize everything: democracy, emigration, matters of agriculture and cattle-raising.[1]

He asks if it were possible to go as a correspondent of *El Nacional* in order that he might pay his expenses. He offers to send information, plans and books and the organization of the patent office along with information about agriculture and machinery. However, in a letter written to Mitre on May 1, 1854, he says that he has given up the idea and will return to Buenos Aires.

From an original letter in the Archives of the Ministry of Foreign Affairs we learn that Sarmiento was first appointed as special envoy and minister to the United States in 1860, and his acceptance outlines his plans. The letter is dated December 29, 1860 and addressed to the acting secretary of state, Norberto de la Riestra and reads as follows:

> The undersigned has received the honorable note in which His Excellency is pleased to advise him of the illustrious distinction with which the President has deigned to favor him, by naming him Envoy Extraordinary and Minister Plenipotentiary of the Republic to the Government of the United States of America. The undersigned in accepting such a delicate charge, permits himself to attribute to an act of pure benevolence of the President the choice that surpasses his merits and capacity, but with the desire of making it acceptable, will do whatever the deep sentiment of the responsibility of the charge depends upon, relying on his efforts and adding to the direct objectives of the mission those studies and tasks that may be useful in the different administrative fields, in a country like ours so lacking in

authorized predecessors, taking from the country of his destination facts, practices and theories that have in their favor the prestige of success which has surpassed all human foresight. Hoping to receive orders and instructions from His Excellency, the undersigned has the honor to present to His Excellency the assurances of his most distinguished consideration and esteem. (Signed) D. F. Sarmiento.[2]

However, nothing came of this appointment since the Senate of the Argentine Confederation, with temporary capital in Parana, on May 28, 1861 refused to approve the appointment. These documents of the Argentine Confederation are in the Archives of the Ministry of Foreign Affairs. (Box 41, File 1, No. 145, Pages 2 and 3)

It is not until July 21, 1863 that Sarmiento was again nominated and the request signed by Bartolomé Mitre and Rufino de Elizalde sent to the Senate for approval reads:

The nomination of an Envoy Extraordinary and Minister Plenipotentiary to the Government of the United States of America being proper to the interests of the Republic, the Executive Power fulfilling what was established in Article 86 sentence 10 of the Constitution, requests the agreement of Your Honor to name Citizen Domingo F. Sarmiento in this position.[3]

The Senate voted its approval July 28, 1863 (Box 41, File 1, No. 147, Page 19), but Sarmiento's letter of acceptance is dated several months later from San Juan where Sarmiento resigned as governor to accept the new position. This part of Sarmiento's life was one of indecision. He was unhappy for more than one reason. He had domestic difficulties that had resulted in a separation. Such difficulties had been brought to a climax with the discovery of letters written by Sarmiento to Aurelia, the daughter of Vélez Sarsfield. Sarmiento was also pessimistic about political events in his province and felt that the idea of naming him to an important post out of the country was only to get rid of him. He wanted to go and yet he didn't. He wrote to Mitre:

My principal ailment of the spirit is that suddenly the

innocent illusions that made me strong until the age of fifty, of not believing in my future or in myself, have vanished. Going to the United States is, then, a rehabilitation and a refuge.[4]

However, on March 3, 1864, Sarmiento accepts the position in a letter to Rufino de Elizalde, Secretary of Foreign Affairs, which reads in part:

In accepting such a lofty mission, will Your Excellency kindly express to the President of the Republic my gratitude for such a high distinction and my fear that despite all the human will can do, it is possible that to carry it out worthily, I may not succeed in following his wishes and all that the interests and dignity of the Republic which I shall have the honor to represent will demand.[5]

A week later, on March 10 he wrote Mitre:

In this state of affairs I, who have many times sacrificed my position to what I believe to be the public interest, would have already renounced the ambassadorship if considerations of — how shall I tell you? — spite, for I cannot find another word, had not detained me. When the Chaco crisis passed I requested to be allowed to indicate the time of my acceptance, refusing the nomination to Chile because I believed myself incapable to fulfill it successfully, and the nomination to the United States, which would give me time to avoid any involvement. Events have gone against me and I find myself having to go against my conscience, which at this very moment tells me I am doing great harm to my native country, leaving it involved in difficulties.[6]

Thus we see the state of mind which possessed Sarmiento when he left Argentina.

His grandson, Augusto Belin Sarmiento, tells that when he mounted his horse to leave San Juan, he looked toward Buenos Aires and remarked to a bystander:

You were fooled! More than ever I shall be President. The

farther away, the more beautiful. They idealize me. . . .[7]

Another time, when Montt had sent him on his trip to Europe and the United States, Sarmiento had felt that it was because it was expedient to send him in order to quiet those who remained. Now, he felt that his friend Mitre was sending him in order to quiet his rivals but he was sure of succeeding Mitre as president. At the same time there were circulating photographs of Sarmiento with the inscription:

Domingo F. Sarmiento, future president of the Argentine Republic.[8]

En Route to the U. S.

Sarmiento arrived in Chile about the middle of April, 1864 where he was to see again many of his friends of other days. In Santiago he saw Montt, Bello, Lastarria and Las Heras and in Valparaiso, he was guest of Mariano Sarratea. He spent happy hours with these friends of his earlier days in exile in Chile and it must be said that he also enjoyed seeing his enemies of old days to show them how far he had advanced, for he was now an international personality and they were still in their modest positions. His mission before the Chilean government consisted in trying to reach an agreement about debts of the war of independence, arranging of boundary limits and to find out what stand Chile was to take in the forthcoming American Congress at Lima. However, on April 14 the Chinchas, islands of Peru, were invaded by Admiral Pinzón of the Spanish Fleet. Such an important event demanded attention and here our new diplomat felt his duty to such an extent that his speech of presenting his credentials was no mere ceremony but rather a dramatic one as the circumstances demanded. This speech was censored by the Argentine Government and from then until he left the American Congress at Lima, he was in difficulties with President Mitre and his immediate superior, Rufino de Elizalde.

Lima Congress

While in Chile, Sarmiento had received an invitation to attend the American Congress which Peru had called, but Elizalde told Sarmiento that the invitation should have been sent to the Argentine Government and not to Sarmiento and that it is not true that the invitation had been lost but rather that Peru hadn't invited Argentina because it was not convenient to invite her. (File, Box 122, p. 18, Congreso Americano) Mitre is also severe with Sarmiento in his desire to attend the Congress and take official part in it saying:

It seems that you might have forgotten the connection of such a congress to which the Brazilian Empire was invited previously and that the United States was excluded because that congress was promoted in hatred of North American democracy, as you well know; therefore we deny this body even our moral support, not only because of this but because this would place us in the dishonorable state of adhering to what others had agreed upon without our being party to the treaty.[9]

However, Sarmiento did go to the Lima Congress and even though he was not the official representative of Argentina and even though he had instructions not to take part in the Congress, he was determined that the Congress should adopt stern measures to meet the emergency that had developed in Peru as a result of the taking of the Chinchas by Spain, and as a result he received many severe letters both from Mitre and Elizalde. Ricardo Rojas treats this difficult episode with a very fair appraisal saying:

After I have examined the documentary sources, the instructions turn out to be precise, both in the case of Chile and in the case of Peru, and if in view of them it appears that Sarmiento went beyond the rules, some communications from the Chancellery, judging his conduct are indefinite and contradictory, doubtless because unforeseen events occurred, like the Spanish attack, and the mails were delayed, events changing, the American participation uncertain; the dealing with the Argentine envoy was difficult, in view of his wilful and saucy character.[10]

Sarmiento was a dynamic but impressionable man. He acted more on impulse of imagination or emotion. In those days he was impressed by several coincidental events. First, the Spanish aggression against Peru and that of France against Mexico; he could see in both events the rise of a European policy of conquest and restoration of monarchy. To all this was added the atmosphere of the American Congress which touched his convictions and the sympathy of Lima which touched his vanity.[11]

In one of his letters to Mitre, Sarmiento describes the warm reception that he had received in Lima and Mitre answers that it seems that the women in Lima have enamored him. Sarmiento answered him in a very strong manner, when we remember that he was writing to the president of the nation he represented.

In a previous letter which I answered at length, you attributed my actions to the desire to win applause in the public square and this in the name of friendship; now it is the applause of the ladies of Lima, something you observe in the name of a few gray hairs you have gotten. Beware of the fascinations of power which make us believe that we are growing in years, prudence and knowledge, while the others are descending in the same proportion until we reach the optical illusion that men, seen from such heights, seem to be mustard seeds. . . . I am in a very good humor and this will not cause me again to take seriously these slips of the pen of your writer. You probably remember when in a committee discussion in the senate you almost told me I was lying, for I answered: "Let's stop the discussion as we are losing our heads; then we shall continue. The opportunity of calling you to order has not yet arrived."[12]

Ricardo Rojas speaks of the polemics between Sarmiento and Mitre, saying:

It is impressive to read that instructive correspondence possible only between two exalted spirits, both patriots though of quite different temperaments. Mitre is the calm architect of a State in formation and Sarmiento is the absent-minded prophet in his unreal or distant, although at the same time true visions. In this discussion both dispense with bureaucratic hierarchy to talk to each other frankly. Both wound each other or reproach each other, but beneath the contradiction lies friendship and above it all shines patriotism with the light of intellectual love.[13]

In the letters to his intimate friend, Jose Posse, Sarmiento shows his feelings about the difficulties that resulted from the American Congress in Lima. On February 4, 1865 he wrote:

> The Argentine government has taken pleasure lately in causing me vexations. . . . I suffer from a misfortune, and that is of having thought, written and worked for twenty years ahead of my followers.[14]

In the same letter he defends his actions at the Congress saying:

> I have sent you two notes asking you to publish the one concerning the Congress. You will be well advised to publish the other on the Spanish-Peruvian matter, because in giving an account of what has been accomplished and without any intention of offering any objection whatsoever, I am following the instructions received on certain dates, days, hours, so that through documents in my possession what you will condemn is the same that they have ordered, and their own opinions without any of mine or a daring step taken in the whole proceedings.[15]

In the last letter before he left Lima, dated April 5, 1865 Sarmiento again says to Posse that he has followed the instructions he has received:

> Thus I received all kinds of instructions, as vague and contradictory as the suppositions from which they came were arbitrary and free. Fortunately I was not at the mercy of such word plays and by giving an account of what has been done, with reference to your orders, I have been able to establish my position as a simple higher official of such a foresighted ministry. I think it will make you laugh to know that they, not I, have done the things that the Spaniards did not do.[16]

In the same letter Sarmiento says that he wants to continue his trip to the United States and speaks of the position the United States is taking in international affairs:

> My whole desire is now limited to continuing my trip to the United States where events lead to a happy conclusion for the Union with great threats of making the Monroe Doctrine effective, which has alarmed Europe very much and above all our French emperor who deifies Caesar, the day the Republic rises, in order to prove that the chief of all emperors was killed, showing that the people, liberty and human destinies can attain their goals without the guardianship of a genius who, for his own good, wishes to cause public well-being.[17]

Instructions for Mission to U. S.

On April 20, 1865 Sarmiento wrote Elizalde that he expected to receive instructions to leave Lima on the arrival of the next ship and that he has therefore decided to leave for the United States on the 28th of April. (Box 122, Document 2, pp. 369-370) Sarmiento had received his instructions for the mission in the United States and I have seen them in the Archives of the Ministry of Foreign Affairs. An extract follows:

> Instructions to His Excellency the Envoy Extraordinary and Minister Plenipotentiary to the Government of the United States of America, Citizen D. F. Sarmiento.
> Article 1. The Argentine Government wishes to cultivate the most cordial relationship with the Government of the United States of America.
> Article 2. Wishes to count on his cooperation to support all that interests the United States of America.
> Article 3. It will be of special attention to Mr. Sarmiento to study and discover what the American Government thinks and does about the question of Mexico and to find out the assurances the Emperor of France has given that Government and these have been that he should not protest as the American Minister in Paris told the Argentine Minister of which fact he will not be able to make use either officially or confidentially with the American Government.

Article 4. He will make an agreement with the representatives of all the Governments of America in Washington on what must be done about the question of Mexico and will send all detailed reports on this matter.

Article 5. The lack of shipping lines (sic) between the United States and the Republic is felt to be damaging to commerce, and Mr. Sarmiento will do everything possible to induce the American Government to establish them by expressing the opinion that the Argentine Government will do whatever it can to protect it for its part.

Article 6. Mr. Sarmiento has the principal mission of transmitting everything that can be of interest to improve and perfect our institutions and develop our moral and material progress, by sending books, memoirs and whatever he believes will be useful to that objective, being careful to ask in advance for the funds he may need.

Article 7. He should also try to make our country known and encourage commerce and immigration indicating the means he thinks necessary to consider, and be careful in his relations with the other diplomatic agents and immigration officials to make known the advantages our country offers.[18]

Sarmiento Arrives

Sarmiento reached New York on the 15th of May, just one month after the tragic assassination of President Lincoln. Of his trip from Callao to Panama and thence across the isthmus to proceed by ship to New York, we know nothing except that in his second letter to Aurelia, he speaks of having endured unspeakable suffering from Panama.

Unspeakable sufferings, since Panama until being in the Fifth Avenue Hotel, were preparing us for the contrast in order to enjoy the life that was going to begin with the sight of all the grandeurs of the land. (XXIX, 28)

In his first letter to Aurelia, written on May 20 Sarmiento tells of finding the deep emotion caused by the tragic assassination of Lincoln and then launches into an impressive description of his feelings upon being back in the United States again.

So many marvels accumulated through wealth, general education and freedom, are beginning to be understood by Europe, whose governments feel small in the presence of the events of the last months, the tragic death of Lincoln having served to give greater solemnity to the abolition of slavery. You will recall my eternal preaching, until your father grew tired, about the United States. I glory in having had twenty years earlier the clear perception of its definitive influence on the destinies of all America and having consoled myself about our depression by announcing to Europe what it is now beginning to feel. You who are young will see the end of the beginning we are now witnessing. (XXIX, 27)

Upon his arrival, Sarmiento had lost one of his trunks and it was the one that contained his credentials. In his first official report to the Argentine government he tells of the loss of the credentials and asks for new ones and his official presentation was thus delayed for some time due to the slow mail service between the two countries. However, it was not Sarmiento's idea to remain in Washington. He went there shortly after his arrival and describes the great parade he saw on the 23rd and 24th of May:

This parade can be characterized as the seizure of the part that the United States plays, namely that of a first class military power in the world, if not the first because of the magnitude of its forces, its inexhaustible resources, its improvements in weaponry and cannons, both on land and at sea. This very new place in its history is being recognized in Europe in the unanimous statements of the press and in the more or less direct declaractions of its governments. (XXXIV, 186-187)

Minister in Washington but Residence in New York

Sarmiento did not make his residence in Washington and even though he has been criticized for this, it is doubtful whether any other diplomat has accomplished so much during his stay as Sarmiento did. Gálvez goes so far as to say:

Argentina while Sarmiento is minister, has no true diplomatic representation in the United States.[19]

However, Sarmiento felt that the foreign diplomats who remained in Washington, idling away their time were overlooking a wonderful opportunity to see the country and learn as much as possible about it. He had definite ideas as to what the work of the legation should be and thought that they should be information centers, giving information about the country represented and seeking to learn the best of the foreign countries. Thus it was that he wrote to Mitre:

> My desire would have been to carry out an old idea of mine concerning embassies, namely to convert these idle factories into work offices, to send out useful information and establish relations more than with governments, with the people.[20]

And he did just that. He lived in New York, where he worked very hard, writing indefatigably. It is almost incredible to believe that he had time to write the long letters he was accustomed to write to his friends, articles for *The Zonda (The North Wind)* *(from a hot, dry wind blowing in the north in Argentina), which he had started again in San Juan, articles for *The Voice of America* *(Latin Americans consider America to be both Americas of the Western Hemisphere), which his Chilean friend, Vicuna Mackenna published in New York, *Both Americas*, the magazine he had hoped would establish contact between the Americas but which was destined for a short life due to the indifference of the South American countries; and besides all of this, books, *Life of Lincoln, Schools as the Basis of Prosperity and of the Republic in the United States, Life in the Chaco*, and *Life of Horace Mann*. In addition he gave many lectures, attended several conventions about education and traveled widely in the country he had so hastily seen twenty years before. Nor did he neglect his diplomatic duties. I have seen the extensive reports sent to the minister of foreign affairs which show that he was interested in everything that would better his country.

Official Reports to the Argentine Government

In his first reports Sarmiento wrote of the enormous war surplus that could be bought for a small sum, recommends torpedo boats, equipment for the Paraguayan War and even that officers, doctors and engineers might come to Argentina to help in the war. Most of the latter had fought on the Confederate side during the Civil War and felt that they should leave the United States in order to begin life anew. Sarmiento offered any and all the prospect of living in his country and wrote many letters of introduction for those who went. Sarmiento was eager to stimulate immigration and wrote an article in the *New York Herald Tribune* about the life of President Mitre. He also sent out reprints of an editorial from the *Standard*, one of the English newspapers of Buenos Aires, saying that there was no better time to emmigrate to Argentina. Furthermore, Sarmiento wrote many articles for publication in the newspapers to justify the Paraguayan War. However, Elizalde, the minister of foreign affairs, felt that the war would be of short duration and wrote Sarmiento on September 26, 1865·

On the subject of war, we have nothing to commission you. Your endeavors are going to be in matters of peace and progress.[2 1]

Other official reports treat of books, education, institutions and economy. One of the important suggestions that Sarmiento sent to his country was about the granting of concessions along the railroad right of way in alternate lots, the system he had seen in the United States. However, this was not used in the railroad from Rosario to Córdoba and in a letter to his friend Posse, written on April 5, 1866, Sarmiento tells of his disgust, which he attributes to political reasons.

I wrote you about changed fortunes. Motivated by a zeal for good, and this being in my instructions, I sent a four-line note to the Department of State, indicating the idea. The Department answered me with one of two pages of polemics to prove that it knew about it and that the laws of the United States had served it as a model when giving the entire railroad line from Córdova to El Rosario to a foreign company. I had to weigh and measure the words of my reply in order not to understand the trivial spirit of these observations that tend only to hold me down, as they say, and to show the truth of the matter. But that note, like the two volumes making up the ones I have sent to the government from Chile, Peru and the United States, will never be published because they are my glory and probably will not contribute much to their glory when compared with the ones I am answering.[22]

County Fairs

Sarmiento visited the county fairs and was thrilled with what he saw. He thought of what his country would be with agricultural implements and education. He wrote the governor of San Juan on October 11, 1865 asking for a thousand pesos or two in gold in order to buy implements:

I believe it will not be excessive to inform Your Excellency that I have advised the Honorable Government of the San Juan Province on a sum of one thousand to two thousand *pesos* to provide agricultural instruments, which serving as a basis for an *Annual Agricultural Fair* can later be sold and renovated for the following year. At present all the States and cities in the United States offer the attraction of their Fairs and Industrial Exhibitions.[23]

English as Means of Progress

At the same time Sarmiento felt the need of teaching English in his country as a means of facilitating progress in education, agriculture and free institutions. He wrote in the same letter:

A voluminous book on education that contains all the information to promote it successfully would be easy to acquire here and would be good as a beginning of a library. Though these books are in English, the poverty of our language is such, that the lessons we need in a language which a certain number of citizens possess, is fearful. It is my opinion that the Government ought to promote the diffusion of English as the only means today of facilitating progress in education, agriculture and free institutions.[24]

Sarmiento Rehabilitated

In a letter written to Posse on February 27, 1866 we can observe the great change that has come over Sarmiento since his arrival in the United States. He had exchanged curt letters with his superiors relative to the Congress in Lima, and Sarmiento, knowing that he would be a candidate for president some day, felt that anything he did was criticized by his rivals for political reasons. However, in less than a year after reaching the United States, absorbed in his writing, working with that inexhaustible energy that so characterized him, he had completed the *Life of Lincoln, Schools as the Basis of Prosperity and of the Republic of the United States* (A book Sarmiento wrote about Education in the U. S.), he had given his famous address before the Rhode Island Historical Society, written numerous articles and letters and he himself knew that he was rehabilitated in his optimistic spirit. He tells Posse that the first thing which helped him was to leave the scene where the troubles were and then he says that it was necessary for him to help himself out of the despondency in which he was:

> Well, I needed to rehabilitate myself in my own eyes and have accomplished this here, by attaining in the opinion of men of some worth and in the press, that approval they never spared me. . . . Here, too, I have come not as Minister Plenipotentiary of Batuecas [*figurative expression for something like our expression Podunk], for our republics sound like such, but as the person I am, and I let them know that, ever since I came, in every work of my pen no matter how insignificant, the Argentine Republic is beginning to be known, esteemed, not because it is worth what it is in the public mind but because, as Suetonius or someone else said, it has persons who can make it worthy.[25]

In the same letter Sarmiento tells Posse how happy he will be to see him come to the United States, if he would fulfill the wish expressed in the last letter. In the next letter Sarmiento again insists upon his coming.

I advise you to come as soon as possible. Here you can find

means and ways of remaking your fortune, entering on your return, with the help of machines, in practical speculations that do not innovate except in the manner and economy of producing what is produced with laborious and rough labor. I insist that you come to see the astonishing machines for wood-working with application to all the usual needs. In Tucuman you have water power and walnut and cedar trees. Here is your capital: as Andreuw said, the work is done by sly, clever machines, that seem to think and almost talk.[26]

Information about Argentina

In the course of carrying out his diplomatic duties, Sarmiento answered many queries about his country. In a letter to Brig. Gen. W. W. Duffield, written on September 29, 1865, (Archives, Box 122, File 1, Page 65-73) Sarmiento gives information about sheep ranching in Argentina and gives a good description of his country at that time. Other tasks that befell the diplomat were answering letters from stamp collectors. When we remember the multiple activities of this tireless man, it is hard to imagine that he would take the time to write a personal letter enclosing an Argentine stamp to an unknown person, giving the historical background of the stamp. An extract of the letter follows:

I remit to you an Argentine Republic stamp, as you request; if in the future I should have some better ones, I shall certainly send them to you. The picture in the center is that of Don Bernadino Rivadavia representing the Washington of the Argentine Republic. He was Secretary of the Junta that proclaimed the self government of the Viceroyalty of Buenos Aires; he was sent to Europe to solicit the aid of England in assuring independence. He was highly esteemed by Secretary Canning; he introduced the representative system, he organized public education and the whole system of republican government. Elected President, he later resigned after having given a consitution, because of resistence of the chiefs of state of the interior to submitting to regular forms, from which started the civil war. He died in Spain in great poverty; and when his party won victory thirty years after his abdication, his ashes were brought to Buenos Aires and received solemnly. All his institutions have been reestablished and his name is that of the Protective Genius of the Republic.[2][7]

Yet in just such simple activities, we can see plainly the mark of greatness. He was putting into practice his ideas of promoting the understanding among peoples. Surely it was of greater value to spend his time in such activities than making formal calls in Washington or attending the social functions of the diplomatic circle in the Capitol. He tells of his long days in New York, when he got up at five o'clock, read, wrote, compiled reports and worked until midnight when he went to bed and slept well, conquering his old insomnia. In spite of his domestic difficulties, the political differences between him and his rivals and moments of genuine sorrow, brought on by the death of his son-in-law and of his son, Dominguito, the years in the United States were years of realization for that dynamic personality that was his. Perhaps it was the many problems that caused him to bury himself in work, or perhaps it was the inspiration that he received from his Aurelia, to whom he wrote:

> Your letter found me, as you were hoping to find me, happy in the country of my choice, happiness brightened by the expression of affection from down there, in the shadowy part of this placid, melancholy, waning moon of mine, and living no longer for myself but to guide others in the darkness of the night. (XXIX, 44)

Friendship with Mrs. Horace Mann

But there was the inspiration of still another woman which spurred him on. Sarmiento had known Mrs. Horace Mann in 1847 during his first trip to the United States when she had served as interpreter for her husband. Sarmiento wrote her shortly after his arrival to the United States to renew their acquaintance. With this letter there began a correspondence which was to last the rest of Mrs. Mann's life. Sarmiento went to visit her in Concord where he passed unforgetable days. She introduced him to the leading writers of the day, Emerson, Longfellow and Hawthorne. She took him to Cambridge, where Sarmiento met the outstanding scientists of the country. He was a guest in the home of the famous astronomer, Gould, whom Sarmiento would later bring to Argentina to open the observatory in Córdoba. Mrs. Mann introduced him to the leading educators, the writers, the officials of the government. Her name opened whatever door for him. She translated *Civilización y barbarie* and part of *Recuerdos de Provincia* into English, and wrote a biography of Sarmiento from information which he himself gave her. Sarmiento said that she would have translated *Viajes* if he had been sure that it would be read.

Mrs. Mann was a charming, cultured woman of about sixty when Sarmiento came to the United States as minister. She had received an excellent education and knew several languages and was vitally interested in education. She and Sarmiento shared the admiration of her deceased husband, Horace Mann, who had done so much for education. Their friendship was without doubt a great inspiration to Sarmiento and he has acknowledged that she was one of the women in his life whose love sustained him. In a letter to Aurelia Vélez, written from Boston on the 15th of October 1865, Sarmiento speaks of Mrs. Mann, an extract of which follows:

Mary Mann is my angel of yore! Her heart leads her. Ah! In the midst of so many disenchantments and treacheries I have the consolation of having been loved by such as you, your father Aberastain, Posse, Mary Mann and a few others. The latter is a victim of a fascination that perhaps comes from an excessive maternal love which overflows her heart, perhaps finding in me an admirer and follower of her husband.

We have seen each other four times in two years but our correspondence is frequent. She outdoes herself for me to help me and protect me. Her first question to anyone who approaches is "Do you know the Argentine Minister?" and the eulogy begins.

She has given me the best friends, introduced me to the highest personages. . . . She admires my *Voyages* and said of *Memories of the Provinces* that she has never read such portraits of life.

My biography takes up all the time her other duties leave her. By next mail I think I can send you the result of her efforts to make me known and esteemed by such notable men as surround her in her new little house in Cambridge where I shall go to see her the day her eldest son receives his degree, or I give thanks for mine. She is close to sixty-one years old and her charm has sway over me to command me to speak English or to distract me from my sorrows. (XXIX, 66-67)

Upon still another occasion, Sarmiento wrote Aurelia about Mary Mann. This time he was en route to Argentina and during the voyage he wrote a diary of some two hundred pages which have been called some of the most revealing pages written. They were dedicated to Aurelia and written in pencil with some drawings. It is indeed fortunate that these pages have been preserved because they give us an intimate glance of Sarmiento in the moment in which he was about to enter upon the realization of his life's dream, to be president of his country. In the diary he tells of having bought a statue of Venus de Milo in Paris, upon which he wrote the following dedication:

"In grateful memory of all the women who loved and helped me in the struggle for life." (II, 293)

Sarmiento enumerated the many women who had loved him, watched over him and guided him. He began with his mother, Doña Paula; then his aunt who took him to live in the home of the priest, Oro, who was to commence the education of Sarmiento; Doña Ángela, who gave him a position as storekeeper; Juana Manso, who shared Sarmiento's ideas and helped him greatly in establishing schools in Argentina; one who is not named who has directed his public acts, and is evidently Aurelia; another who is not named, who was a volcano of insatiable passion, and is believed to be his wife. Then he launches into a eulogy of Mary Mann:

This lady is the incarnation of maternal love. She has left her husband Horace Mann crystallized in the bronze statue that adorns the front of Boston's State Hall. She can be reassured, he will never be forgotten and his sublime glory does not need her protection.

I met her in 1847, at a time when she acted as my interpreter in order to make myself understood with her husband. I renewed my friendship on the occasion of the unveiling of the statue. We then had a common object of adoration. It was necessary to help me accomplish the task destined to me and she began the work. Her life since then is linked to mine though we do not see each other but two or three days a year. Her letters are numerous and the ramifications of her affection include the Argentine Republic because I love it, Juana Manso because she loves me, my daughter because Dominguito, whose picture is on her table and is decorated with garlands of flowers when I go to see her, has died. Wherever I go I shall find friends her solicitude has prepared for me and if something public, like magazines or daily newspapers, speak of the book I can find an unexpected sentence from a letter of mine to her. That writing is hers. (IL, 295)

We know of the high regard that Mrs. Mann had for Sarmiento by her acts of kindness, by her understanding and the many ways she served to inspire him in his work. It is also interesting to note that she wrote on May 20, 1866:

Be assured, my dear sir, that one day your name will be the magic wand which will be working even after your ashes sleep among the remains of your ancestors. (XXIX, 281)

In still another letter, she wrote to Juana Manso:

You will be surprised when I confess to you that I am so presumptuous that I have undertaken to write the biography of our noble friend Mr. Sarmiento. I have been reading his *Voyages*, his book *Civilization and Barbarity*, his noble thoughts in *The Monitor*, *The Annals*, his great work *Popular Education* and I am dejected, as his compatriots have not yet said to him: "Take our hands and do with us what you believe we are capable of doing because your admirable intellectual work, your glories and the distinguished acts of your life give you the power to guide the legislation as well as the education of the people." I have read his *Voyages* as if I were reading a tale of chivalry. With his astuteness of knowledge of what goes on in the high councils of nations, he is so able to understand the power and weakness inherent in government that the reader finds relish while reading. He has told me that his book is little known in his country. I recall that no one is perfect in his own land with honor and glory; that there are few communities which have such a great, good man as he; but his triumphs have been of such nature that I am surprised his books are not read with ardor. I should like to know the thoughts of such a man on all subjects because he is such a profound historian that his less cultured compatriots ought to learn from him all they need to know. . . . As for intellectual culture, I have never seen a more wonderful case than Mr. Sarmiento's, for at a very early age, by himself he has transported himself to each pole of the earth and has understood the politics of nations and the exact reason for their culture and prosperity. What a pity that such a man should grow old! We would need to have him live a few generations to spread the wisdom he possesses. (XXIX, 287-288)

Even more eloquent are the words of Mrs. Mann when she said to Sarmiento:

To me you are not a man, but a nation. (IL, 297)

Not only did this friendship result in Mrs. Mann helping Sarmiento in every way that she could but also in his family. When Dominguito, the beloved son of Sarmiento, died she shared his father's grief and kept flowers by his picture in her home; when Julien Belin died, she invited his wife, Sarmiento's daughter, to come to live with her. She adored Doña Paula, Sarmiento's mother and wanted to know all she could about her. She imagined how San Juan, the birthplace of Sarmiento, must be since Sarmiento never stopped talking of his humble home. She interested herself in all of Sarmiento's plans and devoted herself to helping him in carrying them out. Their monumental friendship stands as an inspiration in the letters exchanged during the rest of her life. These original letters are preserved today in the Archives of the National Library and the Sarmiento Museum. I have seen the original letters of Sarmiento to Mrs. Mann and also have the

Boletín de la Academia Argentina de Letras, which published these
letters. The letters of Mrs. Mann to Sarmiento are in the Archives
of the Sarmiento Museum but I have been unable to see them,
since I have been advised that the archives are not open for
foreigners. However, I have been permitted to work in the General
Archives of the Nation, the Archives of the Mitre Museum and the
Archives of the Ministry of Foreign Affairs, where I have been
given every assistance in my work.

During one of my visits with the outstanding writer, Ricardo
Rojas, we discussed the friendship of Sarmiento and Mrs. Mann.
Dr. Rojas said that the fact that Mrs. Mann was of the age that she
was, that she was a widow with grown sons, all were in favor of
the platonic friendship between the Argentine minister and this
charming woman. He said that the psychological factors brought
into play when a woman has passed the climacteric must be taken
into consideration and that she was a wonderful example of what
a woman can accomplish in using the energies that are released at
this time. He praised Mrs. Mann for her spiritual qualities, her
great understanding and her inspiration to Sarmiento. In his last
book, Rojas said:

> A friendship exemplary for the nobility of its motives, the
> correspondence of both is a beautiful document of
> Argentine-North American intellectual cooperation and a
> platonic relationship between a man and an intellectual
> woman.[28]

In these intimate pages, we can follow the work of Sarmiento
in the United States. From the letters to Mrs. Mann we can learn
of the many plans that Sarmiento was making to better the educational conditions in his country. He had written an article for the
periodical *La Patria* of Valparaiso, Chile, about the seven hundred
teachers who were en route from Boston to the territory of
Washington and who would pass by Valparaiso. In this article he
posed the question of seven hundred North American teachers in
Argentina or Chile, and said that seven hundred North America
teachers would repair in ten years the ruin of three centuries.
Therefore he sought to enlist teachers who would go to Argentina.
He proposed that the brother of Mrs. Mann go to Buenos Aires as

superintendent of schools or director of a normal school and that her son be named as rector of a university to be founded. However, Sarmiento had to wait until later to put into practice his idea of inviting North American teachers to Argentina. Nor were there ever seven hundred, though the figure did reach some seventy, to whom all honor must be given for having left their homes and families to go to a new country to wage war against ignorance. When we consider the fact that these young women went to Argentina, where they had to learn a new language, suffer the hardships of combating all kinds of prejudices as well as enduring physical dangers due to the unhealthful conditions of the country at that time, we must all agree that they share in the glory that is Sarmiento's in having proposed their going to Argentina. Sarmiento must be proud today in that the surplus of teachers in Argentina has been suggested by her government as available for combating illiteracy in the other Latin-American Republics, under the direction of UNESCO.

In a letter to Mrs. Mann written on the 3rd of January, 1867 Sarmiento tells of his impatience because of the time necessary for sending things to Argentina.

> I am notified from San Juan that finally a Chickering piano, two farm machines and others for sewing which I sent them arrived. They took a year or more. I am tired of sending things, books, machines; everything arrives late if not damaged.[2 9]

Nevertheless, he continued sending books to his friends, one of which was a translation of Virgil's *AEneid* by Henry S. Frieze, sent to Dr. Vélez Sarsfield. This book with the dedication signed by Sarmiento is in the Library of the University of Córdoba, where I was shown the copy by the Professor Francisco Jurado Padilla, historian and author of several works including one about Sarmiento called *Sarmiento y Vélez Sarsfield*.

Campaign for President

Besides showing us a beautiful friendship based upon the efforts of each to aid the other in their common zeal to further education, and Mrs. Mann's interest in making Sarmiento and

Argentina better known in the United States, the letters of
Sarmiento and Mrs. Mann also give us a good picture of the
progress of Sarmiento's candidacy for president in his country. We
know that when Sarmiento had accepted the mission to the
United States, it was not without some misgivings. He felt that his
rivals wanted him out of the country in order that he would not
become president. It is not certain just how his name began to be
mentioned as a candidate, but Rojas says that it was inspired by
the personal suggestion of Sarmiento's dearest friends, Dr. Vélez
Sarsfield in Buenos Aires and Jose Posse in Tucumán. Gálvez
declares that it was suggested by Régulo Martínez of San Juan
upon the suggestion of Sarmiento himself and backed by the
enthusiasm of three women, Juana Manso and Aurelia Vélez
Sarsfield in Buenos Aires, and Mary Mann, who thought that he
should return to Buenos Aires to fight for the cause, either with
permission to leave his position in the United States or resigning it.
However, the most interesting part of his candidacy is that without a party, without any organization, and away from the
country, Sarmiento began to be talked about as the next President. On January 3, 1867 Sarmiento wrote to Mary Mann:

> The correspondence that reached me yesterday from Chile
> confirms all the previous letters. It is believed the election
> will be unanimous on the part of all the Provinces and all the
> parties. Perhaps a rival candidate will not appear. Does this
> activity not seem strange to you? In Chile, Peru, Brazil
> articlés are appearing in newspapers and single sheets
> supporting my candidacy. . . . Everyone who has some hope
> supports me. In any case, this nomination of an absent
> person, who offers *to teach people to read* as his whole
> program, will always appear as a sign of consolation.[30]

When he was sending Mary Mann notes for his biography,
Sarmiento refers to the intrigue that surrounded his appointment
saying:

> Make them believe as a joke that this is the intention of my
> friends on placing me in such a respectable position when the
> United States serves as a model for all countries, and the one
> who for so many years has made them an object of study will

return to his country to put into practice the lessons of such a rich experience.[31]

Sarmiento's relations with Mitre's ministers, Elizalde, Rawson, Gelly y Obes, had definitely cooled since the time that Sarmiento was governor of San Juan and since his mission to Chile and Peru. Having been discredited both in the war with the Chacho and in his activity in the American Congress at Lima, Sarmiento felt hurt and declared that there was personal hostility back of the official acts. In December 1866 when there arrived the notice that he was to be changed from minister in the United States to minister to Chile, Sarmiento again felt that such a proposal was to prevent him from accomplishing what he had set out to do in the United States and he proposed to resign his position or go to Buenos Aires to thwart the plans of his rivals. He wrote to Mary Mann:

What a singular situation is mine! I am at the mercy of my opponents and for five years caught in their nets![32]

Rojas analyzes the situation saying:

They did not know what was better to do with this man: whether to elevate him or attack him, to have him near or far, as friend or enemy. He was alert in his New York lookout, sensitive to all rumors that reached him from his country. He aspired to the presidency, confident in himself and in Providence in which he believed so firmly. And he was bound to believe in it because his candidacy was prospering by itself despite so much hostility.[33]

But the news from his country discouraged him. Contradictory information, late in arriving due to the slowness of communications in those days, kept him continually upset. Besides the war with Paraguay which continued, there were uprisings in the provinces. Sarmiento saw that the country was returning to the bloody days of the civil wars and felt that all his work had been in vain. He wrote Mrs. Mann:

You can imagine that at my age I now lack energy to undertake anew the struggle against the barbarism of our ignorant popular masses.[34]

In another letter he said:

> We will have to fight for years against the barbarism shown by bosses like López and Urquiza who know how to win, get rich and command by means to which the Indian and Spanish elements in our populated centers so easily lend themselves. I have to think of some way to save from shipwreck the ship of state, already dismantled and sunk. In such a sad state of affairs as at present it is almost impossible to think of my candidacy which needs a base to introduce new elements of life and culture.[35]

His pessimism was such that he could not return to his country. He said:

> With my recent loss, my years, and distance, I suffer from disenchantment that is the ultimate form of sorrow. If these sad forebodings should come to pass I would have to think of choosing occupations and a country in which to end my days. All South America is a chaos, Mexico does not come out of it and in the United States I would not know how to live because I lack the North American character to make my way.[36]

Sarmiento Visits Paris Again

From the middle of June until early in August 1867, Sarmiento was away from the United States on a trip to Paris to see the World's Fair. In a letter to Mrs. Mann before sailing he mentions that he would have liked to have received the honorary degree of which she had written, but that it would be well at any time and produce its effects. We know that Sarmiento went to Paris to distract his attention from the bad news that he had been receiving from his country and also to be in Europe again to see at first sight the opinion of Europe at that moment when France had been repelled in Mexico and Spain in Peru. This information would be necessary to him, should he be elected. He saw his friends of his first trip and spoke with Thiers about American problems. The Argentine residents in Paris greeted him cordially and a poet that he had first known in Montevideo on his trip to Europe in 1846, Hilario Ascasubi, who had also taken part in the campaign with Urquiza against Rosas, wrote a poem to Sarmiento as a toast at the banquet given him on the Fourth of July. His days were full, seeing all that he could of the Fair and the great improvements in Paris since his first visit twenty years ago. He saw his old friends and the Argentine residents in Paris and from them he learned that his candidacy was almost certain. He wrote to Mary Mann upon his return:

> There the thought and the desire that I should return soon to my country was unanimous. My correspondence and that received by everyone here announce as a *humanly* possible fact that I shall be called quite soon. The movement is general in all the Republic, in the army, and in the cities according to what they write me, the adversary parties are in agreement only on this point of my nomination.[37]

But upon his return from Paris, Sarmiento received a letter from his daughter, Faustina, which described the situation in the country in somber tones and advised him to decline the nomination for the presidency. In the reply, we can see that Sarmiento realizes the difficulties that will be his, but he will face them as his civic duty for his country. The letter is as follows:

> I have gone through terrible trials such as few men have probably experienced. Finally the measure of suffering reached its peak and now I find myself with a more decisive state of mind.

> Our country is like other countries upset by pestilential fevers, subject to an endemic illness, civil war, uprising of the uncivilized in Paraguay and in La Rioja (Andean province).

> My mission was since youth to fight it with books as in *Civilization and Barbarity*, with a sword as at Caucete, with education as in the schools.

> In this terrible battle have perished my son, Soriano, whom I educated and loved so much, my nephew Marcos, my beloved friend Aberastain and San Juan which is also dear to me.

Fortunately for the peace of my conscience not one, not even San Juan, has suffered through my fault or compromised positions or interest by my advice. Each one acted through his own feelings and his own ideas.

If as you tell me my compatriots believe I am the anchor of salvation for the Republic and would want to entrust to me the power to exorcise so many evils, far from fleeing such a position, as you advise me, considering the quiet, respectable post I have here which Mrs. Mann describes to you, I would fly to wherever the will of my compatriots should call me, not to enjoy honors which are not so great as is believed, but to put my shoulder against the building that is collapsing, to work humbly and valiantly like the poor little fellow from San Juan when he saw the city threatened with being swallowed up.

The curses of some, the insults of others, will be my reward but I have faith that never did abandon me, that with work, decision, knowledge of the evils of the country and their causes, we can finally succeed in lifting our country, elevating it at least to the state of those who count themselves civilized.

This is the effect of your letter upon me.

You must arm yourself with courage like your father who accepts life as it comes to us without believing you have a right to happiness, which has been denied to us.

Why would you be happier than your country? Now, then, let's put an end to tears!

Be my daughter in all that, in suffering, working, hoping for tomorrow or beyond the grave; you, in another better life you hope for, I in the pages of history which is the heaven of public men.

Julio will be cured of his moral illness. I am certain. Your father, *Sarmiento*[38]

In a letter to his friend Posse, Sarmiento continues his ideas as to what he will do if he is elected:

An election held as it appears up to now, by a spontaneous act of opinion would place at my disposal an immense moral power. It is necessary to keep that character in it; and as I do not wish to rule but to *govern* and put into effect the thoughts I have set forth for thirty years, I need to be carried into power by a strong opinion in order to put my hand where it hurts. Already the old time soldiers in Buenos Aires can tell where the shoe pinches. The men of the Mazorca Society (against the tyrany of Rosas), barbarians, thieves, understand me. For my part and this I tell only to you, if they let me I shall give American history a page. Thirty years of study, travels, experience and the sight of nations other than those made up of villages, have taught me much.[39]

The news from Buenos Aires was better. The wife of President Mitre had written her son, Bartolito, employed in the Argentine legation that the candidacy of Sarmiento was the most popular. Juana Manso told him that the discussion in the newspapers was lively and that he would win. Lucio Mansilla, the nephew of Rosas, whom Sarmiento had first known on his trip to Europe in 1847 and who had later become an intimate friend of Dominguito, had written Sarmiento his famous letter saying that there were many sympathizers in the army and asking him to speak for himself. Some of his friends advised him to return to Buenos Aires, but Dr. Vélez Sarsfield thought the time has not yet arrived for his return and furthermore thought that Sarmiento should not write since his reply to Mansilla had been resented by Mitre. To soften this blow, Dr. Vélez told Sarmiento that there were no readers worthy of him in the country. Even his former superior, the minister of foreign affairs, Rufino de Elizalde, who had resigned, wrote Sarmiento:

As soon as the war is over, which will be soon, revolutionary groups will be finished and the electoral crisis will become calm. It is not yet easy to foresee which candidate will win; probably it will be you or I. Some are for Alsino, but I think he will not have more votes than some people here and if the war ends before, not even that. Dr. Vélez is also mentioned, but he does not even have support. I tell you this with reservations. I believe I shall be sending you very important news by the next mail packet.[40]

In January 1868 Sarmiento was elected national senator by

the legislature of San Juan, but he neither accepted nor resigned this honor. Perhaps he was waiting to see what results another election would show. At any rate, his absence from the country permitted him to delay action. Later, in the same month, Mitre appointed Sarmiento to his cabinet as minister of interior. This Sarmiento refused to accept because he did not want to be an official candidate endorsed by Mitre since Elizalde was criticized for this. President Mitre was very busy with the Paraguayan war, but he could not but take notice of his successor. In a letter from Tuyú Cue which Mitre himself called his "political will," Mitre states his impartiality in the campaign between Elizalde and Sarmiento but disapproves of Urquiza and also takes José Hernández, the future author of *Martín Fierro*, to task for his article against Sarmiento. However, Sarmiento was not content with Mitre's stand and wrote to Mary Mann:

> It is a poor document. You do not know if he is in favor of me or of Elizalde.[41]

But as Rojas points out, it is exactly this that makes the document so important. Sarmiento wanted his election to be a result of a spontaneous vote on the part of the people, and he didn't want to be criticized for being an official candidate; therefore, the stand that Mitre took is truly just.

> This was an injustice of Sarmiento, since Mitre's merit in that piece of work consisted in not saying if he was in favor of one or the other and in letting the public elect a president without official imposition and armed conflict. What more could he want? Mitre fulfilled that promise. Posterity considers historical that document which to Sarmiento seemed poor. Thanks to him, the hard to please man became president.[42]

During all the while the political campaign for his presidency was raging, Sarmiento never left his work. He continued his writing, his travels in the United States, his visits to educational conventions, his efforts to contract teachers to send to Argentina, as well as scientists, his collecting of books and information to send to his country and his ceaseless activity of learning all h could to take back to Argentina.

Receives Doctor of Laws Degree from Michigan

Before he was to realize his life long ambition of being elected President, he was to have another desire realized, that of receiving an honorary degree of Doctor of Laws. From his letters to Mary Mann, we know that it had been spoken of before he went to Paris. However, from his account to her written on the same day, it would seem to have come as a surprise. Irving Leonard has described this happy event saying:

> The University records shed little light on the circumstances which led to the granting of a degree to Sarmiento, though it seems probable that the devoted friend of the Argentine statesman, the widow of the great American educator, Horace Mann, had some influence in the matter. On page 273 of the *Proceedings of the Board of Regents*, 1864-70, there appears the brief statement: The President announced the special order assigned for 2 o'clock P. M., being the consideration of conferring honorary degrees upon several persons. On motion of Regent Gilbert the degree of Doctor of Laws was conferred on Domingo F. Sarmiento, Envoy Extraordinary and Minister Plenipotentiary from the Argentine Republic.[43]

Sarmiento wrote Mary Mann on June 24, 1868:

> I came to Ann Arbor to accompany Mitre, who had made an engagement with a young lady to attend the exercises and commencement. I attended, seated on the left of the President on the platform. The diplomas were distributed, and you can imagine my surprise on hearing the President say that the Board of Regents was awarding the degree of Doctor of Laws to Dr. D. F. Sarmiento for his services lent to Education in South America![44]

Sarmiento also briefly mentions the ceremony at Ann Arbor in his diary written en route to Buenos Aires and dedicated to Aurelia, whom he had not seen since 1861.

We had promised to meet at commencement at the University of Michigan. On the 24th when the commencement exercises were over, the group of professors, students and guests went to a church prepared for the occasion; on the platform the President had Gen. Pope on his left and the right was designated for me. Among the names of those who were receiving the degree of Doctor of Laws, mine was pronounced by the President with a short speech in which he praised my good services to the cause of education in America. I recall that in Chile in fifteen years and in my country in eight years my name does not appear in public print.

I am an old acquaintance of the University of Michigan, and its library contains half a dozen of my writings. I am, then, a doctor like Longfellow, John Stuart Mill and others who each in his own field were granted that degree.[4][5]

Courtesy the National Archives of Argentina

Sarmiento and the Embassy staff in Washington, 1865.

However, the most complete description of the important event is found in a letter from his secretary, Bartolito Mitre y Vedia some eighteen years later. It is easy to imagine that both Sarmiento and his secretary had been bored with the ceremony, because Mitre says that after the presentation of the diplomas to the graduates and to the others honored with degrees, he supposed that the ceremony was ending and he was not paying attention but rather was looking around at the 1500 in the audience, when he suddenly heard the president pronounce in a loud voice and in an English pronunciation: Domingo Faustino Sarmiento, Ambassador from the Argentine Republic and the president-elect of that nation. Mitre says that although Sarmiento was a good translator of English and wrote it well, in fairness to the truth, he didn't speak it well or understand it perfectly. Mitre describes the scene with great feeling in his letter written in 1885.

The president said, more or less, that he had the honor of presenting to the audience His Excellency the Minister Plenipotentiary of the Argentine Republic, Mr. Domingo Faustino Sarmiento, diplomat by chance and schoolmaster all his life, a man to whom the cause of education in America owed most important services and whom his fellow citizens had just elected President of the Republic in recognition of those services, which spoke very highly in favor of our country that in this way rewarded those who dedicated themselves to the cause of teaching by contributing powerfully to the intellectual progress of nations and, as a result of this, to their material progress.

The speaker added some allusion to his plan to take American men and women teachers to the Argentine Republic and then, picking up a diploma from the table, said that the University of Michigan, wishing properly to honor their worthy guest and indicate as an act of public distinction his visit to that remote region of the United States to attend that festivity, had decided to grant him the title of doctor, because those who teach are doctors, and he invited the audience to stand to salute the tireless worker for education in South America, future President of the Argentine Republic.

I would have given anything if those who laughed at the Michigan doctorate could have been present at that moment in the auditorium at Ann Arbor.

They surely would not have laughed at the homage paid to our country in the person of one of its most distinguished men more than two thousand miles away, amid the acclamation of the audience, while the musicians were playing *Hail, Columbia*, the popular hymn of the North American people, and while everybody was shaking hands with us as a token of fraternal good will.

I do not know what was happening to you although I can imagine it, recalling how your hands were trembling as you held the diploma the President had just given you in the presence of the standing audience, but as for me I must say my heart was pounding, and I did not sob out loud because those things you cannot do in public; nevertheless, it was hard for me to behave correctly.

And here is the good part.

I translated for you as best I could the words of the president of the University, and when I had concluded, in a voice that at first was out of tune, shall we say, but which bit by bit grew calmer and more energetic, and growing enthusiastic you said something to me like this, the details of which I remember vaguely, even though the general idea has remained perfectly engraved in my memory.

"Kindly express my gratitude in my name and that of my country for these sincere demonstrations. Tell them that above all I have been a school teacher during my life no matter what position I occupied, until the highest one, and that today as the representative of the Argentine Republic abroad I continue to be mainly a school teacher. Tell them . . ."

"But, sir . . . "

"that down there in South America we are learning lessons in good government in the great school of the United States, and in order to make the best of them we teach citizens how to run a Republic, and as they prove worthy of it, we take the North American public school to the borders of our immense countries where . . . "

"But how shall I be able to . . . "

"where if the fact of democracy is not yet a complete truth, we are moving toward that goal with sure steps, building imperishable foundations that are not upsetting, nor will they upset, our ardent struggles, to the point where there is always an idea and teaching although sometimes we take the wrong path, seeking through mistaken ways, sometimes unconsciously, thinking we are pursuing hapless momentary goals but actually transcendental victories — objectives that are sooner or later achieved and are incorporated forever into our national life like other essential elements of the politico-social organism, which in fifty years of . . . "

"I do not know, sir, what I am going to do to say all that; the people are waiting."

"Tell them we are a young people, almost children, who have had to do and redo everything in our short national life, children of a power that failed to give us or teach us what it did not have for itself, nor even knew, being in this situation more unfortunate than the children of the Puritans, who inherited teaching from which they have been able to profit splendidly, not having to exchange the rough Colonial dress for the proud tunic of democracy in their own government, to travel over half a continent in years and years of constant battle and tell them . . . "

"Sir, they are waiting for us!"

"Finally, tell them that if they were happier than we in having ancestors among those who fled the religious persecutions of the reign of James I and established in New England with religious freedom the foundations of political freedom, when our independent life came into being, we have not left behind grave problems for the future which, like the problem of slavery, could only be solved according to laws of humanity and progress at the cost of thousands of lives and many millions of *pesos*."

"If you will allow me . . . "

"That as soon as we shook off the rude yoke of our valiant conquerors, our first laws assured forever liberty for all men who inhabit our land, opening to all the world's flags our great river arteries whose sources, like those of the Nile, in some of them disappear into unknown regions where man has not even been able to go to search for them, and they established . . . "

"If you please, sir, I am going to say a few words."

"Assure them that if my fellow citizens honor me with their votes, in order to rule the destinies of the country I shall be in the presidency of the Republic as always, above all, a school teacher."

I waited no longer. I stopped, said a few words thanking them, as had been requested, for the honor that was being given to Mr. Sarmiento, and I think I inserted in my Ollendorf (grammar) English something of Don Domingo's speech which I do not pretend to have stated faithfully after so many years have passed since that memorable day when emotion and fright prevented me from fixing in my mind what was buzzing around me.

I do indeed remember that they applauded me very much, I do not know whether because I ended quickly, which must have been very pleasing to the audience, tired of sitting, or because I touched the patriotic fiber of those present, a sure means of being very successful in such situations even though it be playing the organ.

With these reminiscences I have tried to show that if there are well-earned titles in life and by any concept a man can feel satisfied, that if his attainment is linked in other respects to such solemn and pleasant moments as those, when his patriotic heart and mind of a thinker poured over my poor individuality in torrents of fervent eloquence, which were unfortunately lost in that vacuum of my inability at that moment to translate to the audience which you would have electrified with your words, that title is one that with so much honor to you and your country was conceded to you in the quiet, picturesque city of Ann Arbor. This is the day about which I have tried to give a brief idea, with the deficiency resulting from the unusual circumstances of the traveler with no resources to authenticate his facts, and so many other things to keep him busy. (XXIC, 382-385)

The University of Michigan might well be proud of having been the first and only institution to bestow upon Sarmiento the long coveted degree of Doctor of Laws and thus demonstrated at an early date its recognition of the cultural ties that exist between the peoples of the western hemisphere. Sarmiento did not forget the honor done him, and in the *Proceedings of the Board of Regents* (page 369) the thanks of the Board are rendered to President Domingo F. Sarmiento for the presentation of two very rare South American curiosities. These "curiosities" are described elsewhere in the same volume (page 361) in the report of Professor Alexander Winchell upon contributions to the museum, as follows:

(1.) A fine specimen of the Cóndor of the Andes, (*Vultur gryphus*,) which, when living, probably measured nine feet from tip to tip of the wings.
(2.) Chlamyphorus truncatus, (Harlan.) A unique species of the family of armadillos, from the mountains of Chili (sic), of which only one specimen is known to have hitherto reached North America, while only one exists in Europe.

It is of interest to note that of these two gifts the Armadillo is still numbered among the rarities of the Museums' collections.[46]

Receiving the degree of Doctor of Laws from the University of Michigan was most gratifying to Sarmiento, who had coveted such a degree for many years. In 1853 he had written from Santiago to the president of the Chamber of Justice in Buenos Aires asking that he be given the degree in virtue of having defended the liberty of the Argentine Republic for some twenty-five years, citing his *Commentarios* for his thesis and asking why he should be deprived of the degree because his parents had been too poor to send him to the university. He says that the universities give degrees to students who have not even reached the full development of their ability and that it is the obligation of the university to recognize in certain instances those who would have obtained degrees in their youth if they had been able to attend the university. He reminds the president of the Chamber that the celebrated university of Oxford had thus honored the printer Benjamin Franklin. With his clever pen he says that if it is true that he does not possess the wisdom that Franklin had, it is also true that the university of Buenos Aires is no Oxford. He continues:

That Argentine wisdom I promote, that law I defend, those institutions I comment upon, that freedom I support, that culture I disseminate, owe me nothing. So! Such persevering efforts, a life dedicated to the public cause, do they not require stimulus, approval, title, at a time when the burning passions of youth have already lessened? (XV, 366)

Sarmiento Leaves the U. S.

The elections had been held, but the results were not yet known when Sarmiento decided to leave. He says that his return home had long been planned but that he was waiting for a certain letter in order to time his journey home. He describes his preparations for leaving the country, where he had spent more than three years, in the diary that he wrote aboard the *Merrimac* for his love, Aurelia, whom he had not seen for seven years, saying:

On this trip I propose to describe the traveler as the sole protagonist; this reading, dedicated to you alone, gives assurance that to complete the idea, every hour of the day you will be present in my mind. I shall live, then, anticipating your presence, and each scene I describe will have you as a spectator pleased to receive this daily tribute.[47]

Sarmiento says that his circle of friends in the United States was so large that taking leave of them in itself was a serious undertaking — that he had them in Chicago, Cambridge, Washington and Lancaster — in three directions and hundreds of miles apart. But he had traveled widely in the United States and loved the country and there was another friend of whom he spoke.

But besides I have a tender and constant friend whom I wanted to see, in all her attractiveness, in case I never see her again. Nature in the United States is so beautiful, so smiling. I went to say farewell to the Hudson, to say farewell waving my hand to each of its picturesque views. I wanted to hear the roar of Niagara Falls if only for a minute, and since my last visit to the West had been in winter, wrapped in cold sheets of snow, that picture was stereotyped if it were not to be refreshed, enhanced by the green vestments of spring.[48]

Sarmiento said good-by to Chicago of which he said:

Every day Chicago is taking on more and more the rank of the center and capital of the United States.[49]

Sarmiento admired Chicago very much. He had written to Juana Manso in 1866 that New York seemed to be an old city, without life alongside Chicago with its vitality and its population, which doubled every four years.

Here God is greater than in other places, or man is greater than all the human race. (XXI, 142)

Here he had known, thanks to Mary Mann, Mrs. Kate N. Dogget, who had shown him the vast city with its museums, schools and university. Here, too, he had known the Wickershams, a superintendent of schools in Pennsylvania, and his brother and their wives. Sarmiento says that he first dared to speak English with them,

For ten days the four of us dined, ate lunch and supper together, which makes thirty English lessons, for this was the first time I ventured to speak it. (IL, 298)

Of a trip to Chicago in the winter to see it in its winter dress, Sarmiento said that he had enjoyed that visit immensely:

That was a time of activity and the most complete and lively happiness I have had in the United States. (IL, 299)

The last night that he was in Chicago, he saw a gigantic parade of the Germans celebrating their *Sängerfest* with forty thousand torchlights. He was greatly impressed with this sight, which reminded him of the torrents of lava pouring from Vesuvius. He describes the torchlight parade, saying:

This is a torrent of humanity, with flames of fire, for when you look ahead or behind the column, they come together and present one surface of fire. The Milky Way is pale and far away.[50]

When he went to Cambridge, where he also had many friends to take leave of, he was visited by Dr. Hill, the president of Harvard College, Professor Gould, the famous astronomer, who would later go to Argentina to open its first observatory in Córdoba during Sarmiento's presidency, Ralph Waldo Emerson, and the other Emerson (the philosopher), Dr. Allen of the *Christian Examiner*, and several other ladies and gentlemen invited by Mrs. Mann to a farewell tea in his honor. He says:

Boston and Cambridge are, then, crowned with lights like Chicago in this last proof of stereotype prints.[51]

Sarmiento was criticized for not living in Washington but he had his reasons. He preferred to go to Washington from time to time, but he spent the most of his time in New York writing. He also traveled widely and attended educational conventions, where he formed an active part since he was named to work on various committees. Thus he was putting into practice his ideas of promoting understanding among the people instead of spending his time in Washington playing cards with the diplomatic corps. He speaks of his opinion about what a diplomat should do in his diary to Aurelia and his many activities in the United States are an eloquent proof in themselves which need no defense.

I had to say good-by to the President in writing since I have no letter of retirement. I said what I needed to Mr. Seward to satisfy him for not having resided in Washington. If the mission of a diplomat is to cultivate good relations, I have fulfilled mine more than abundantly. One does not esteem what he does not know, and I have devoted money that another person would have invested in meals and a carriage, in traveling around the United States, studying its institutions, visiting its public establishments, mixing with the people while the diplomatic corps plays cards in Washington.

Not only the European ministers do not know what the United States is after ten years of residence, but those from South America do not return home more advanced (in knowledge of the U.S.)

I shall make this country known in mine and our relations will always be congenial.[52]

Sarmiento describes the last preparations for leaving the United States. He says that there are only two occasions in life in which he puts all his faculties of mind and body into play — when campaigning and when traveling, that in the former it is necessary to overcome fatigue; in the latter to make provision for all contingencies. We can imagine this man of genius as he collected his belongings and the accumulation of things that three years in the United States would cause, together with the last minute purchases.

I use all my faculties of body and mind in only two situations in life; in military campaigns and on trips. To show that I am superior to fatigue in one case, foresee everything in the other case — this is my vanity and success. Later I give in to laziness and let my life run wherever it wishes. What does it matter to me?

Before a trip I am a general, a diplomat, an impresario Nothing is left to be done or arranged, not even the imaginary.

This time orders given are not taking long to be carried out. Thanks to the perfection and speed of the Adams Express, a million dollar enterprise for sending packages and messages, from Providence a box of china, from Cambridge a copy of *Civilization*, etc. arrive. The binding is dripping wet.

The ship from Rio de Janeiro brings correspondence that seems to arrive in time to resolve doubts. The fourth and last issue of *Ambas Américas* is published and bound barely twenty hours before departure. The Police Department, Land Office and Health Department send the requested reports after a time, and by the minutes and hours packages of books, clothing and travel articles arrive.

At twelve the trunks are closed, they are on board at two, the anchor is lifted at three. All my friends accompany me. Mitre, hearing the signal to set sail, throws himself upon my neck and amid sobs, — crying like a child says: "See my mother, speak to her a lot about me." This filial tenderness, desire to console her, would gain him pardon for all his faults. Here one does not have to pardon.[53]

And thus it was on the 23rd of July 1868 that Sarmiento sailed on the *Merrimac* for Buenos Aires, leaving behind the United States, where he had spent three active years as the Minister Plenipotentiary of his country. Even though the results of the election were not officially known, he had received letters stating that he had won in the interior. He could not bear to be away from the theatre of events of such importance and had decided to return to his country whether or not he was elected President. He had written to Mary Mann on the 5th of May 1868,

I have made up my mind to leave in June whether I be president-elect or senator, for in case I do not receive a majority vote I wish to save the government from anarchy and realize some of my ideas.[54]

If the first visit of Sarmiento to the United States had been the turning point in his life, the formation of his philosophy based upon what he had seen so briefly in his quick trip, then the second visit of three years was just as important in its influence upon Sarmiento. Here he was to see in operation many of the ideas he had predicted twenty years before, and he was happy to have had the foresight about the great republic he so admired. These three years were the best apprenticeship he could have as a prelude to the presidency which awaited him upon his return. Ricardo Rojas describes the three years of Sarmiento as follows:

> The three years Sarmiento lived in the United States as a diplomat were serene, pleasant, beneficial, but not the happiest in his life. Travels, studies, honors filled his curiosity and vanity to the brim. Salcedo, Halbach, Lavalle, Bartolito, the four young men employed at the legation, surrounded him with affection. He delighted in his friendship with Mrs. Mann and his relation to his kind English teacher; yet none of that lessened his loneliness or the silent anguish of his soul. Dominguito and Don Julio Belin, his daughter's husband, had just died. Nostalgia for his country and political ambitions reduced to uncertainty from a distance did not agree with his character.[55]

2. Impressions of the Second Visit

Sarmiento had arrived on May 15, 1865 for his second visit to the United States. Again he landed at New York and we know of his first impressions from a letter he wrote on the 6th of June to his beloved Aurelia.

> A volume would be needed in order to communicate my impressions of two weeks' residence. It is a life summed up in hours as in the delirium of a fever. It is Satan's temptation showing the kingdoms of earth from a high mountain.

> Unspeakable sufferings since Panama until reaching the Fifth Avenue Hotel prepared us by contrast to enjoy the life that was going to begin with the sight of all the grandeurs of the land.

> I shall give you an idea of the spectacle without details and as much as a letter permits. I am also sending the letter from

New York City, which now includes Brooklyn as a district on the other side of the Hudson, a district that has 370,000 inhabitants, and New Jersey on the other side of the navigable river which gives the city as its main square the beautiful bay and as countryside, planted with palaces, all the territory this side of it to the Atlantic.

Such are the changes experienced since my first trip that the part of the city I now live in and the most luxurious did not exist then. The magnificent avenues that divide this part are forty yards wide with seven yard wide sidewalks and trees on the sides and railroads in the center. The cross streets measure only twenty yards with shady parks at short distances. Broadway, which is being planned for seven miles, is fifty yards wide, and for more than a mile is bordered by marble, granite, stone or brick mansions, palaces for hotels with a thousand guests, print shops, banks, stores, clubs, associations. Broadway is today unrivalled in the world for its architectural luxury and its activity. There are accumulated the great fortunes that are going to be spent on Fifth Avenue, another street of mansions like in Genoa or the St. Germain section of New York.

Recently they put in prison a lady who has in this street a residence worth 160,000 *duros* (five pesetas to the duro) kept up with appropriate pomp and acquired through thirty years of practicing the innocent profession of securing abortions.

This amplitude of the streets, that vegetation of trees, bushes, flowers and vines which do not cover the stupendous buildings but adorn them, the confusion of coaches, buses, trains, people, posters and signs cause a strange impression to those like us who used to live on twelve-feet-wide streets, which limit one's vision.

Greenwood, or New York cemetery, is the wonder of the world; a huge garden with lakes, mountains and marble decorations. It is superior in beauty to Central Park, although the latter has already cost twelve million *duros* though it is still just a nursery. On Saturdays three or four thousand de luxe carriages drive along its roads. A commission with powers given by the legislature makes laws, directs the work and has its own police and funds (income). (XXIX, 28-29)

Washington

In the same letter Sarmiento tells of going to Washington where he saw a parade of 200,000 men.

A unique sight in history, a river of men, horses, cannons, guns, that paraded by companies for two days, the army having been ordered to bring rations for two days in order to provide for the difficult task of feeding that enormous mass of human beings! (XXIX, 29)

Sarmiento says that the public greeted the victorious chiefs and their battalions with frantic applause.

On the day following the parade, Sarmiento was admitted to the military court which was trying the assassins of President Lincoln and which he describes.

The following day I was admitted to the confines of the Military Court where the murderers of the glorious Lincoln are on trial; the criminals in front of me: Mrs. Surrat, who was the *soul* of the plot, Payne, whom nobody can determine just who he is nor what his name is, Dr. Mudd and the rest. The English judicial system is very impressive. The criminals, always present and accompanied by their lawyers, hear the testimony of the witnesses, can by cross-examination question them in turn. That day negroes made statements, a new thing in the country as formerly they could not be witnesses, and I was suddenly moved by a *zamba* (person of Indian and mulatto mixed race) who, asked if she had been a slave, answered with emotion: "A slave, yes, but now I am free!" (XXIX, 30)

From Washington, Sarmiento visited the war torn city of Richmond, where he says he visited the ruins by moonlight. Later he visited other sites of the recently terminated Civil War, including

Fort Stegman, where he says "the fate of four million slaves, the future of the Republic, the independence of America and perhaps the liberty of the world was decided!" (XXIX, 30) Sarmiento observed at first hand the battlefields and describes them saying:

> In the space of a half block that at this point divides the two lines, you cannot take a step without stepping on a bomb fragment, a cut off shotgun, boots with legs (in them), cartridge belts, heads, cannon balls, rags of uniforms . . . horrors! (XXIX, 30)

Hotels

In this same letter Sarmiento continues his impressions of the many sights he was seeing. He was impressed again as upon his first trip with the fine hotels — and mentions the elevator in a special way.

> Two days later I was in Baltimore, a day later in Philadelphia with six hundred thousand inhabitants, wondering if New York is a more beautiful city than these and if its hotels can stand alongside the Continental, where three times I had to be conducted to my rooms, lost in that colossal labyrinth until they showed me the furnished room that takes you from the first floor to the seventh, letting off on the intermediate floors passengers who go up and down sitting on soft seats. (XXIX, 30-31)

The speed and movement of travel impressed Sarmiento, who said, "I see that I could never finish, although I am flying as I write you, just as people fly around here in trains and ships." (XXIX, 31)

Travel Difficulties

But not all is comfort, Sarmiento says, as he describes the difficulties that he encounters in his travels, for you will get a seat only if you are quick enough to grab one.

One feels he is living, or rather life invades him, moves him, drags him along, a life of material and intellectual enjoyments and of constant activity. It has its difficulties. You travel from one palace to another to live on four *pesos* like a prince, with a bathroom next to the bed, five meals a day, rooms for reading, smoking, reception, barbershops, telegraph, everything at hand. On the other hand, from one palace to another a railroad or ship carries you, and that is the cause of my anguish. Imagine what life would be like if God had entrusted us with keeping in motion our hearts upon which life depends. We would die at the least distraction. Well, this is what happens on trips. The person who was a prince at the St. Nicholas or Continental Hotel descends to the state of peasant, of a bundle, on trains and ships. He probably will have a seat if he was clever enough to reserve one. If not he will, like all the Argentine legation (did) from Baltimore to Washington, have to settle in one coach or another while it rains, at night, and at twenty-five or thirty miles per hour. He will probably sleep in a berth if he can get one by standing in line for three hours, and will eat if he has good fists and strong elbows to struggle to make his way to the diner.

There is no possible claim or distinction of persons or classes. It would be ridiculous to invoke the title of diplomat among these well informed, rich, patient, quiet country bumpkins who are resigned to these inevitable inconveniences of building up life in minutes and flying through space while cutting out distances. (XXIX, 31-32)

Sarmiento continues in his letter to Aurelia telling her that the one solution to the difficulties in traveling is to travel with a lady, since there is a special door to the dining room reserved for ladies, special coaches for ladies and their companions and that staterooms are not given to men until the ladies are accommodated. "And what ladies! All country girls, even in faces and costumes much like your own friends when you go to the country villa." (XXIX, 32)

Sarmiento says that he positively must find a lady companion to travel with, and he renews his invitation to her, saying that he would be happy if she could persuade her father to come.

Oh, if you could persuade the doctor from Córdoba to take a four-month trip to this delightful country, how much he would enjoy himself seeing the wonders of the most advanced civilization, the whirlwind of public life, business, press, telegraphs and ships which swarm here just as wagons do back there: admiring the work of God in bays, lakes, forests and rivers and that of men in institutions, cities, inventions, books, schools and amazing riches! But that is like preaching in the desert. (XXIX, 32-33)

His Prophecies Fulfilled

In his letters to Mary Mann, Sarmiento also expresses his wonder at the changes in the twenty years since his first visit. In a letter written in May 1866 discussing his book *Viajes* with Mrs. Mann, Sarmiento says:

But few have seen in them as you have, the traveler capable after twenty years of measuring and understanding the glorious future of the Republic. Then you recall the Europeans themselves, except Tocqueville, ridiculed the progress of the United States. The book by Morton Peto, much more direct than my traveler's tale, is now saying what I said twenty years ago.[1]

Chicago

In the same letter to Mrs. Mann, Sarmiento describes his impressions of Chicago and says that the farther inland you go, the greater is the development of the Yankee genius, which has changed the direction of the Chicago river.

I am in Chicago enjoying the pleasures of living in continual amazement, seeing the wonders accomplished by industry, liberty and intelligence. The Yankee genius is developed in inverse proportion to the square of the distances from *the coasts*! The farther you go from European contact the greater the fund of *Yankee notions* becomes, and with more ease. There is a property common to the human race that we call *common sense*. Common sense is the sum of notions beyond doubt that we have of truth. *To go upstream*, for example, is to go against the nature of things. Who would conceive the idea of making a river flow in the opposite direction from its current? Well, there is a project here to make the Chicago River flow from Lake Michigan instead of into it as it has been doing since the beginning. I find it more difficult to imagine the idea than of executing the plan, because *common sense* opposes the idea. This character is observed in many American inventions, repeating the spirit of that circumstance the fact that only in the ancient Romans and in modern convicts was there any equal in my observations as a traveler.[2]

But Sarmiento is sad when he compares the conditions that he sees in the Far West with what exists in his own country because he says that he will not have time to apply in his country all the useful ideas that he has.

The sight of the rapid development of this former Far West and new center of the United States sickens me when comparing it with our own backwardness under the same circumstances, and while hoarding all the useful ideas I am gathering, I am saddened: to think that *I am on the way to becoming an old man* and will not have sufficient time or energy to apply them to the development of my country.[3]

In still another letter to Mary Mann, written from Saratoga Springs in July 1866, Sarmiento refers to his prophetic vision in his book *Viajes* about the United States.

I marvel at the changes that have happened in these twenty years since I traveled through the same part of the country. How much power and wealth! Have you read in my *Voyages* the part (I cannot point out the page) in which it announced within twenty years (1847) the elevation of the Republic, by the United States? I recommend to you that passage and take note of the prophecy foreseen to the day and hour.[4]

The Mid West

Sarmiento was a good traveler and was continually seeing all that he could. When he went into the Middle West to attend the teachers' convention in Indianapolis in September 1866, he describes his impressions with the keen observation with which he was gifted.

"On the other side of the Allegheny Mountains the new world begins . . ." (XXIX, 179)

> From Pittsburgh I go on to Columbus, capital of Ohio, from Columbus to Indianapolis, capital of Indiana, and end my trip at this time. You go from one capital to another: the train swallows up the intervening distances by the hour. I have an unquenchable curiosity. Probably nobody has seen more than I though many may have traveled more. I see that in the crowds traveling with me. They talk, read, sleep: only I am glued to the train window from dawn to dusk, looking with a steady gaze, seeing forests, corn, potatoes, little houses, factories, towns, waterfalls go by, always watching, looking, happily, silently, in a contemplative mood. Thus I have acquired the faculty of seeing, measuring, comparing, observing, contemplating, remembering. All the trees new to me attract my attention, and if a small weed is from my country, I greet it as I pass like a friend. If I get lost in cities while wandering through the streets it is enough for me to notice the thousands of signs, printed pictures; then I recognize one that I noticed an hour earlier that lacked the top of an "A", or a picture of Lincoln or Grant located on the right, and this is enough to direct me because I had looked carefully at everything: signs, pictures, architecture. (XXIX, 182)

Sarmiento has already spoken of his admiration for Chicagc and again he writes of the energetic new city:

> The aristocracy of the young Herculean city is made up of schools and elevators; its princes are Universities and the Astronomical Observatory, and the Opera the most sumptuous in the United States; the plebeians are the hotels, factories, mansions, clubs, and hundreds of churches. (XXIX, 187)

Another of the sights in Chicago which impressed Sarmiento was the water-works, of which he says: "A tunnel two miles long seeks clean water in the heart of the lake to provide the city, and I have walked through a gallery seventy feet under Lake Michigan. (XXIX, 189) While Sarmiento was in Chicago, the news reached him that the municipality of Buenos Aires was trying to install a water-system. He therefore engaged the services of the engineer who had just completed the famous aqueduct in Chicago and arrived as president in time to inaugurate the system in Buenos Aires in September 1868, where he gave the inauguration speech. (Ct. XXI, 249) Sarmiento also noted the tunnels under the Chicago River, the revolving bridges that interfere with traffic as they are constantly having to open for the endless procession of ships that come and go, the vast elevators which swallow up a whole trainload of grain in fifteen minutes and in a little longer time deposit it into the holds of the ships loading on the other side of the river. Having visited the Middle West upon his first trip and thus seeing the growth of the cities in twenty years, Sarmiento compares their progress with that of South America.

What is being done in South America while this is happening here? Pittsburgh, Columbus, Indianapolis, Chicago, Milkane (???) (Milwaukee?), a hundred cities, riches and products accumulated in one hundred years are demonstrating contrary to extenuating circumstances of routine that we are not following the right path, for the farther we advance on the wrong path, the farther behind we will remain, and that is the sad thought which the sight of what I see in this region, which even now smells like a burnt forest, like a land recently uprooted, suggests to me. (XXIX, 190)

The Stockyards

Another excursion took Sarmiento to the celebrated Chicago stockyards.

Another trip to the famous stockyards of Chicago, the salting places of Buenos Aires. They are a city of wood for the sale of cattle. Three hundred acres of fields are set aside to protect the pavement from snow and rains. Thirty yard streets divide blocks with names and numbers. An artesian well provides water for ten, twenty, one hundred thousand inhabitants: steers, sheep and hogs. A hotel like the Fifth Avenue in New York with a capacity of fifteen hundred guests shelters cattlemen and buyers, a bank like the Bank of London contains the millions that pass from one hand to another every day. Nine railroads are connected with this city of domestic animals and take them to the slaughter house, because their graces do not walk on their legs as in uncivilized countries; they would lose a few pounds of fat or would never become tenderfoot hogs who cannot move. (XXIX, 191)

But there in Chicago Sarmiento also found a familiar sight — cattle that resembled that of Argentina in the midst of the fattened herds. He tells of his experience and finds that Texas is a province of Argentina.

"How is the cattle in your country?" a cattle raiser from Michigan was asking me. "Well, it is big, bony cattle with longer legs than this cattle, with twisted horns; how can I describe those animals of my country, so ordinary compared with that Michigan stock that is well-trained, has friendly eyes, is fat, tame, fleshy, with tiny shanks and short legs. "Look," I finally say to the inquisitive fellow, "it is like that bay colored steer in those trappings," to speak in the technical language of my country, that was pounding heavily on the wooden pavement and seemed to greet us with its tender, quiet look as it passed in front of us. "Of course," the man answered, "because those steers are from Texas." I had no words to express my delight! Spaniards, then, my compatriots!

Texas, in case you do not know, is also a province of the Argentine Republic. There are ranches covering ten miles, properties with one hundred thousand heads of cattle worth three pesos per cow with calves. There are ranchers, that is, *gauchos* on horseback, and you cannot find milk for tea in many places, and butter is brought from other states. Most of the inhabitants are poor, there is much meat, there are few schools, dirty villages, rags everywhere and the shiny knife (drawn) at every curse word, and the Texans were the first to rise up against the Government and the last to submit.

Happy is the one who can recognize the cause of things! The same at both ends of the earth!

This is the way it was in California; such were the cattle, the ranch, the inhabitants, but the law of North American lands went there, divided the soil into lots and a nation arose in ten years and today eighty boats are loading wheat in San Francisco for London. (XXIX, 191-192)

New York and Farewell

In his travel diary written aboard the *Merrimac*, we read the last impressions of Sarmiento about New York.

New York seen from the bay lets you understand that this is the future queen of the seas, just like sailing around the lagoons of Venice you feel that the body of the queen of the Adriatic is buried there.

When within a year the railroad of the Pacific, Yeddo, Yokohama, Peking, Melbourne is finished, promissory notes will be signed in New York for London, Liverpool and Paris.

But for the traveler, New York must be seen while entering from the sea, not while leaving. When the spirit is half salty at the sight of the ocean, it can sense the new life which that surprising bay inspires, where you enter through an opening which enormous fortresses enclose and guard. From there two miles of palaces, forests, cottages, mansions, factories, all green, painted and shiny attract one's glances from the tiny settlement of Coney Island to that of Staten Island.

When he landed in Boston, Dickens said that he was surprised to see a suckling child, for the paint on the houses is so fresh that it seems as if there had not been time for children to be born.

These outskirts of New York seen with field glasses resemble those landscapes on a fan, ever smiling, with Greek vases, Armida palaces, rosy young shepherds who are always dancing.

Staten Island is a large island with big homes and playgrounds. I spent two days there before sailing to renew my impressions and to say farewell to Mr. Davidson and that bedecked nature.

Farewell to the United States! I take them with me as a souvenir, as a model. They are the Hudson, Staten Island, Niagara, Chicago as nature. They are Mrs. Mann, Davidson, Emerson, Longfellow and as many noble personalities as men. The Republic as an institution. The future of the world is a promise. Farewell, farewell, farewell![5]

All the admiration and love that Sarmiento felt for the United States is summed up in this emotional farewell. He was sad at leaving as if he knew that he would return no more.

3. Influence of the Second Visit

Sarmiento returned from the United States feeling that he had spent the years there for a good reason — to be able to fulfill better the duties that awaited him in his country. In a letter to his friend, Lucio V. Mansilla, written from New York in September 1867, Sarmiento wrote:

Perhaps my residence in the United States in such an instructive age, the years and a life that can be called honest, give to my message of advice or my actions the authority they formerly lacked because they could not be considered the fruit of experience. (IL, 268)

And for Sarmiento, he had the secret of the success of the country he so admired in one word: education. At the meeting of the Indianapolis Teachers' Convention in August 1866, Sarmiento had said:

The greatness achieved by the United States is a cause for admiration by the other states, but men who cannot be in a permanent state of admiration, immediately examine and will soon discover the secret well-spring, the regulator of this energetic machine which is none other than the general diffusion of education and the spontaneous, persevering efforts of good citizens to spread it. (XXI, 240)

One of the books written during his stay in the United States, *Schools as the Basis of Prosperity and of the Republic in the United States*, was written in order to implant the ideas for which he had worked all his life. However, this book was little read since the entire edition was lost in a fire in the government building. He had boasted when he received the honorary degree from the University of Michigan that he was a school teacher and that if he were elected president of his country, he would continue being a school teacher. Therefore it was a moment of great emotion for Sarmiento when he was welcomed by the teachers of the public and private schools of Buenos Aires. He had been proud of the welcome given him by the population of Buenos Aires, but of this welcome he said:

But the welcome of teachers and school children is not the same. This is purely mine; this I yield to no one because it belongs exclusively to me, because it is the result of my thirty years of work. (XXI, 244)

In this same speech Sarmiento answered the jeering of an opposition newspaper which had asked:

I wonder what Sarmiento will bring us from the United States if he is elected President? And the same person answered: "Schools, nothing but schools!" . . . When that newspaper said I would bring only schools from the United States it was telling the truth because I come from a land, gentlemen, where education is everything, where education has managed to establish true democracy by making races and classes equal. (XXI, 244-245)

This was to be the program of Sarmiento:

For that purpose we need to make the entire Republic a
school. Yes! a school where everyone learns, where all
become *educated* and form a solid nucleus that can sustain
true democracy which makes for the happiness of republics.
(XXI, 248)

In the United States Sarmiento had seen that the majority of
the teachers are women, and he paid tribute to women as teachers.

I come from a country where there are ninety thousand
women school teachers and ten thousand men school
teachers because education is entrusted to the woman as
more competent, more capable of directing the hearts of children. Men teach only certain subjects.

The mission of woman as an educator is set for her by nature
because she has more heart; married or unmarried, she has
maternal instinct in her bosom. Man cannot do that because
his education, no matter how complete it may be, does not
give him the feelings nature gave to woman. (XXI, 248)

Sarmiento believed so strongly in the mission of the woman as
teacher that he began during his presidency to contract women
teachers from the United States to staff the normal schools of
Argentina. These young ladies were selected with the help of Mrs.
Mann, and tribute must be paid such courageous teachers who
went from their home and country to be builders with Sarmiento
of the Argentina he dreamed of. Some seventy teachers went to
Argentina, many of whom never returned home. Of all it is said
that they were loved and honored by the country they went to
serve.

But it was not schools alone that Sarmiento brought from the
United States. In addition, he wanted to encourage immigration
and to make the foreigner into an Argentine. He believed that one
of the greatest sources of strength in the United States was the
powerful influx of immigrants, none of whom claims his former
citizenship upon being received into the great nation.

The United States with a population of fifty million, receives
from one-half to the one million foreigners a year, but that
million are North Americans from the time they arrive be-

cause it does not occur to any of them to call themselves English or Swedish in the presence of the majesty and grandeur of the power that welcomes him into its heart. (XXXV, 290)

One of Sarmiento's projects when he was Senator of the Province of Buenos Aires in 1858 had been the establishment of the agricultural colony of Chivilcoy. Now, upon his return from the United States, it was one of the first places he visited, and here it was that he gave the economic aspects of his program.

Well, here I am in Chivilcoy, the Pampa as it can be in ten years. Here is the Argentine *gaucho* of yesterday with a house to live in, a piece of land to let him produce food for his family; here is the foreigner already domesticated, more owner of the territory than the very inhabitants of the country, for if he is poor it is because he has no set profession; if he is rich he lives in the city of Buenos Aires.

I say this to all the people of the Republic, that Chivilcoy is the program of President Domingo Faustino Sarmiento, Doctor of the University of Michigan, as I have been called in jest. (XXI, 266)

Ricardo Rojas says that Sarmiento was influenced by Lincoln's example as President. He proposed to finish the disorder that hindered the development of his country, and from his biography of the great Civil War president, there is no doubt that Sarmiento could profit from the example of Lincoln.

Naturally he brought schools, because since his youth he took them with him wherever he went, but he also brought the principle of authority founded in the presidential power according to our Constitution and invoked the example of Lincoln during the War of Secession, at the conclusion of which he was present. He had also written a biography of the late President Lincoln.[1]

Sarmiento compares the impressions that he had of his first trip to the United States with those of Charles Dickens, who was

there at about the same time. He is always pointing to the
prophecies made in his book *Viajes* about the United States.

> In the scientific, warlike, economic campaign the free
> Argentines undertook to re-establish the ideas of
> representative, republican, federal government which as we
> have seen was reduced to a red flag and the cry "Death to the
> savages, disgusting, filthy unitarians" as the whole constitu-
> tion, in 1859 a loose-leaf book appeared in the pages of a
> newspaper to be circulated in the Argentine provinces,
> making known the real United States, by a traveler who had
> traveled through there at the same time and perhaps in the
> same months as Dickens, both running across each other in
> the same places. Dickens took to England some sarcastic
> comments and satires which included details of customs,
> while the political traveler brought to his country the revela-
> tion of the greatness attained through liberty and the first
> ideas on federal government. (XXXVIII, 286)

To the charge that he wished to *norteamericanizar* his country,
Sarmiento says that the blame should not be placed upon him but
rather upon the Constitution.

> Let our Constitution, not us, be blamed for this tendency.
> The reporting member of the original Confederation, Dr.
> Carril, in presenting the plan said that it had been inspired by
> that source, renouncing the Swiss system as inapplicable to
> us. The Informant Member of the reforms presented by
> Buenos Aires assured the Convention that his effort had been
> to adjust the old one even more to the prescriptions and
> practices of the North American Constitution. Much can be
> opposed to this system which, according to the speech of Dr.
> Vélez, imposes a sort of servitude on our spirit, let us say,
> shackling it in its flight and its freedom of opinion according
> to the dictates of what we believe is our reason. But peace of
> conscience is better in order to continue with such already
> routine success, and to accept school teachers and ancestors
> who attempt in vain, every ten years, the creation of a
> government of which we do not know how it will work nor
> do we know what the results of a mistake will be. (XXXIX,
> 691)

However, Sarmiento can't escape the charge so easily, for there are many opinions as to his being influenced by the United States. Arturo Capdevila, one of the outstanding modern writers of Argentina, says that it was in the United States that Sarmiento reached the stature that was his. "There was where his soul reached its giant greatness. He observed, contemplated, meditated. He who is great understands very well his greatness."[2]

Ricardo Rojas says that it was in the United States that Sarmiento learned to be a statesman.

In order for that son to make a true man of America, he had been preparing himself since the time he fought the *caudillos* [bosses] in Cuyo, since he wrote *Facundo*, since he traveled the civilized world to study government and education. Teacher and writer in Chile, he had later made his apprenticeship as a legislator in the State of Buenos Aires and as governor of San Juan, but in the United States he had learned to be a statesman through the knowledge of its institutions, schools, progress. Democracy and the federal representative rule that he already knew in 1849 and 1854 according to his own admission, were the object of more calm study in active practice for thirty years in the United States, where he found the experimental basis of his doctrine in evaluating man through work, culture and liberty.[3]

Narciso Márquez, Director of the Mitre Museum and well known historian and scholar, says of Sarmiento and the influence which the United States had upon him:

Sarmiento gave preferential attention to the United States. He did this understanding the great organizing ability of its citizens, comprehending their theoretical, practical but creative talent, and also because of their great scientific faculties, already outstanding in the times of Sarmiento. All this, joined to the great Americanist spirit of the illustrious son of San Juan, despite a universalism, worthy of him as of one who believes he is a universalist in the world of ideas, art, sciences and everything that constitutes useful creations for the good of society.[4]

FOOTNOTES
PART ONE

Chapter II

1. Stuart Edgar Grummon, A Sarmiento Anthology, Princeton, 1948, p. 101.
2. William Henry Hudson, *Far Away and Long Ago*, New York, pp. 16-17.
3. This reference and others similarly indicated are to Sarmiento's *Obras*.
4. Lucio V. Mansilla, *Una excursión a los indios ranqueles*, Buenos Aires, 1939, I., p. 30.

Chapter III

1. Alberto Palcos, *The Pan American Ideals* of Sarmiento, Buenos Aires, 1938, p. 5.
2. Ricardo Rojas, *El profeta de la pampa*, Buenos Aires, 1945, p. XII.
3. Ricardo Rojas, *El pensamiento vivo de Sarmiento*, Buenos Aires, 1941, pp. 18-19.
4. Alberto Palcos, *Sarmiento, la vida, la obra, las ideas, el genio*, Buenos Aires, 1938, p. 16.
5. Ricardo Rojas, *El profeta de la pampa*, p. 6.
6. Rojas, *El profeta de la pampa*, p. 26.
7. Rojas, *El pensamiento vivo de Sarmiento*, p. 29.
8. Palcos, *Sarmiento*, pp. 70-71.

Chapter IV

1. Archives, Ministry of Foreign Affairs, File No. 53, Note No. 86, Buenos Aires.
2. Alberto Palcos, *Páginas confidenciales de Sarmiento*, Buenos Aires, 1944, pp. 35-36.
3. Gaspar Mortillaro, *Sarmiento, Anécdotas de su vida*, 1938, Buenos Aires, p. 60.

4. Rojas, *El profeta de la pampa*, pp. 246-248.

5. Rojas, *El profeta de la pampa*, p. 276.

6. Manuel Gálvez, *Vida de Sarmiento*, Buenos Aires, 1945, p. 177.

7. Palcos, *Páginas confidenciales*, pp. 41-43.

8. Rojas, *El profeta de la pampa*, p. 279.

PART TWO

Chapter I

1. Rojas, *El profeta de la pampa*, p. 316.

2. Museo Mitre, Buenos Aires, *Al Lector americano*, original manuscript, pp. 6-7.

3. *Ibid.* p. 9.

4. *Sarmiento - Mitre Correspondencia 1846 — 1868*, Buenos Aires, 1911, p. 30.

5. *Ibid.* p. 66.

6. *Ibid.* p. 99.

7. Rojas, *El profeta de la pampa*, p. 316.

Chapter II

1. *Sarmiento — Mitre Correspondencia*, Buenos Aires, p. 50.

2. Archives, Ministry of Foreign Affairs, Caja 41, Legajo 1, No. 145, Folio 1.

3. Archives, Ministry of Foreign Affairs, Caja 41, Legajo 1, No. 147, Folio 3.

4. *Sarmiento — Mitre Correspondencia*, p. 218.

5. Archives, Ministry of Foreign Affairs, Caja 41, Legajo 1, No. 147, Folio 10.

6. *Sarmiento — Mitre Correspondencia*, p. 281.

7. Augusto Belin Sarmiento, *Sarmiento anecdótico*, Saint Cloud, 1929, p. 192.

8. Gaspar Mortillaro, *Sarmiento, Esquema Biográfico*, B. A. 1938, p. 101.

9. *Sarmiento — Mitre Correspondencia*, p. 302.

10. Rojas, *El profeta de la pampa, p. 467.*

11. *Ibid.* p. 469.

12. *Sarmiento — Mitre Correspondencia*, p. 339.

13. Rojas, *El profeta de la pampa*, p. 471.

14. *Epistolario entre Sarmiento y Posse*, Buenos Aires, 1946, p. 143.

15. *Ibid.* p. 144.

16. *Ibid.* p. 147.

17. *Id.*

18. Archives, Min. For. Af. Caja 122, Año 1864, Folios 2-4.

19. Gálvez, *op. cit.* p. 389.

20. *Sarmiento — Mitre Correspondencia*, p. 364.

21. Archives, Ministry of Foreign Affairs, Caja 122, Legajo 4, Folio 103.

22. *Epistolario entre Sarmiento y Posse*, p. 164.

23. Archives, Ministry of Foreign Affairs, Caja 122, Legajo 1, Page 80.

24. *Loc. cit.*

25. *Epistolario entre Sarmiento y Posse*, p. 161.

26. *Ibid.* p. 163.

27. Archives, Ministry of Foreign Affairs, Box 122, File 1, Page 43.

28. Rojas, *El profeta de la pampa*, p. 481.

29. BAAL, III, No. 9, 1935, p. 94.

30. *Ibid.* pp. 93-94.

31. *Ibid.* pp. 95-96.

32. *Ibid.* p. 92.

33. Rojas, *El profeta de la pampa*, pp. 484-485.

34. BAAL, III, pp. 9, 96.

35. *Ibid.* pp. 78-79.

36. *Ibid.* p. 98.

37. BAAL, IV, pp. 15, 482.

38. Julia Ottolenghi, *Sarmiento a través de un Epistolario*, p. 72.

39. *Epistolario entre Sarmiento y Posse*, p. 171.

40. Archives, Ministry of Foreign Affairs, Caja 122, Legajo 4, Folio 151.

41. BAAL, III, No. 9, p. 78.

42. Rojas, *El profeta de la pampa*, p. 490.

43. Irving A. Leonard, "Sarmiento's Visits to North America," *Michigan Alumnus Quarterly Review*, July 24, 1943, Vol. XLIX, No. 24, p. 324.

44. BAAL, IV, No. 14, p. 345.

45. *Palcos, Páginas Confidenciales*, pp. 139-140.

46. Leonard, *op. cit.* p. 325.

47. *Palcos, Páginas Confidenciales*, p. 136-137.

48. *Ibid.* p. 137.

49. *Ibid.* p. 138.

50. *Palcos, Páginas Confidenciales*, p. 139.

51. *Ibid.* p. 142.

52. *loc. cit.*

53. *Ibid.* p. 152-153.

54. BAAL, III, pp. 11-12, 377.

55. Rojas, *El profeta de la pampa*, p. 492.

Chapter II

1. BAAL, III, 9, p. 86.

2. *Ibid.* pp. 86-87.

3. *Ibid.* p. 87.

4. BAAL, IV, No. 15, p. 474.

5. *Palcos, Páginas Confidenciales*, pp. 153-154.

· Section 3.

1. Rojas, *El profeta de la pampa*, p. 521.

2. Arturo Capdevila, "Sarmiento en los Estados Unidos," *La Prensa*, June 19, 1948.

3. Rojas, *El profeta de la pampa*, p. 520.

4. Narciso Márquez, letter to author, October 19, 1949.

BIBLIOGRAPHY

1. Editions

Complete Works

Sarmiento, Domingo Faustino, *Obras de Domingo F. Sarmiento*, Santiago de Chile, Imprenta Gutenberg, 1885-1903, 53 Vols.

Sarmiento, Domingo Faustino, *Obras de Domingo F. Sarmiento*, Buenos Aires, Moreno, 1900, 53 Vols. (Separate works)

Vol. II — *Artículos críticos y literarios*, 1841-1842, 1842-1853

Vol. III — *Recuerdos de provincia*, Biografías, 1885

Vol. V — *Viajes por Europa, Africa i América*, 1845-1847, 1886

Vol. VII — *Civilización y barbarie*, 1896

Vol. X — *Legislación y progresos en Chile*, 1896

Vol. XI — *De la educación popular*, 1896

Vol. XII — *Educación común*, 1896

Vol. XV — *Las ciento y una*, 1897

Vol. XXI — *Discursos populares*, 1899

Vol. XXIX — *Ambas Américas*, 1899

Vol. XXXIV — *Cuestiones Americanas*, 1900

Vol. XXXVIII — *Conflicto y armonías de las razas en América*, 1900

Vol. XXXIX — *Los doctrinos revolucionaries*, (1874-1880) 1900

Vol. XL — *Los desfallecimientos y los desvíos; política de 1880*

Vol. XLV — *Antonino Aberostain, Vida de Dominguito*, 1900

Sarmiento, D. F., *Cartas de Sarmiento a la Sra. María Mann*, BAAL, 1935, III, 1936, IV, 1937, V.

Sarmiento, Domingo F., *Epistolario entre Sarmiento y Posse*, B. A. 1946 Museo Histórico Sarmiento V 1 — Edited by A. P. Castro.

Sarmiento, Domingo Faustino, *Sarmiento — Mitre; correspondencia 1846-1868*, Buenos Aires, 1911, 382 pages.

2. Studies

Belin Sarmiento, Augusto, *Sarmiento anecdótico*, Saint Cloud:

Imp. Belin 1929, 335 pages.

Capdevila, Arturo, *Sarmiento en los Estades Unidos*, La Prensa, June 19, 1948.

Gálvez, Manuel, *Vida de Sarmiento, el hombre de autoridad*, Buenos Aires, Emece, 1945, 679 pages.

Guerra, J. Guillermo, *Sarmiento, su vida i sus obras*, Santiago, Imp. Elzaviriana, 1901, 359 pages.

Grummon, Stuart Edgar, Alison W. Bunkley, *A Sarmiento Anthology*, Princeton, 1948.

Leonard, Irving A. *Sarmiento's Visits to North America*, Michigan Alumnus Quarterly Review, July 24, 1943, Vol. XLIX, No. 24, p. 324.

Mortillaro, Gaspor, *Sarmiento; esquema biogrático yanecdotos de au vida*, 1811-1888, por J. V. Gonzales, Buenos Aires, Ed. Araujo, 1938, 160 pages.

Ottolenghi, Julian, *Sarmiento a través de un epistolario*, Buenos Aires, 1934.

Palcos, Alberto, *Páginas confidenciales de Domingo F. Sarmiento*, Editorial Elevación, Buenos Aires, 1944.

Palcos, Alberto, *Sarmiento: la vida, la obras, las ideas, el genio*, Buenos Aires, El Ateneo, 1938, 351 pages.

Palcos, Alberto, *The Pan-America ideals of Sarmiento*, Buenos Aires, Inst. Cultural-Arg. N.A. 1938, 20 pages.

Rojas, Ricardo, *El profeta de la pampa; vida de Sarmiento*, Buenos Aires, Editorial Losada, 1945, 728 pages.

Rojas, Ricardo, *El pensamiento vivo de Sarmiento*, Buenos Aires, Ed. Losada, 1941, 254 pages.

3. Other Studies

Holmes, Henry A., *Martín Fierro, an Epic of the Argentines*, N.Y. Inst. de los Espanos en EE.UU. 1923, 177 pages.

Hudson, Wm. Henry, *Far Away and Long Ago*, New York.

Kirkpatrick, F. A., *A History of the Argentine Republic*, Cambridge, 1931.

Kirkpatrick, F. A., *Latin America*, N.Y. MacMillan Co. & Cambridge, Univ. Pr. 1939, 456 pages.

Levene, Ricardo, *A History of Argentina*, Chapel Hill, U. of N.C. Press, 1937, 565 pages.

Mansilla, Lucio V., *Una excursión a los Indios Ranqueles*, Buenos Aires, 1939.

Robertson, W. S., *History of the Latin-American Nations*, New York, 1932, pp. 299-335.